War in the Pacific:

End of the Asiatic Fleet

The Classified Report of Admiral Thomas C. Hart

**With a Biography of Admiral Hart and Foreword
by Charles Culbertson**

**Clarion Publishing
Staunton, Virginia**

To the memory of
Robert D. Byrnes

Table of Contents

Illustrations

Foreword

The book you are about to read was originally a classified military report on the run-up to war in the Pacific by Admiral Thomas C. Hart, the last commander of the Asiatic Fleet. The confidential report – portions of which were labeled "Secret" – was written by him after he was recalled to the United States from the Pacific in 1942. He fashioned the report from personal diary entries and scattered Asiatic Fleet documents he had in his possession. Everything else of an official nature had been destroyed by the Japanese.

A copy of the report was discovered in 2002 in an auction of the effects of the late Robert D. Byrnes of Connecticut, a political reporter and editor for the *Hartford Courant*. In the late 1940s, Byrnes borrowed the declassified original from the office of naval records for a newspaper project, photocopied it, and then tucked the copy away. It is seeing the light of day, in its entirety, here for the first time.

Admiral Hart's report – originally titled "Narrative of Events, Asiatic Fleet, Leading up to War and From 8 December 1941 to 15 February 1942" – actually begins long before the Japanese attack on Pearl Harbor. The admiral presents an overview of the military and political situation throughout the Far East as it existed up to June 1, 1941, and then follows the rapid descent into war in chronologic installments. Admittedly, his narrative leading up to the start of the war is hardly gripping; he relates in detail the intricate maneuverings of the Americans, Dutch, British, Australians and Japanese, touching on what seems to be every dispatch, every movement of the fleet, every provisioning of ships and shore batteries, every dispute between military and political representatives, and so on. But what that portion of his narrative lacks in drama it makes up for in sheer information. Thanks to the personal records Hart kept, we have a rare, detailed picture of what was going on in the Asiatic Fleet's sphere of influence in its last months of existence.

Naturally, the admiral's account of the war itself makes for much more interesting reading. While he was in no way a dramatic writer, Hart was educated and expressed himself clearly and intelligently. His account of the Japanese onslaught in the Far East and the frantic, often frustrated attempts of the Asiatic Fleet to counter it – or to at least slow it down – is measured yet fascinating, and full of facts that otherwise might have been lost.

Hart rarely inserted himself or his views in the narrative, but every now and then he couldn't help himself. Of particular interest is his less-than-enthusiastic view of the performance of Dutch Rear Admiral Karel Doorman, whom Hart considered "over-apprehensive of enemy bombing" and "a very cautious sea commander… not inclined to take commensurate risk." He noted that "Only war proves what is correct and what is wrong, who is effective and who is not."

Also of interest is his mention of a situation that is still familiar to the United States to this day – what Hart called "a natural tendency (on the part of allies) to hold back and expect American surface forces not to hold back."

And this about the enemy: "Nothing is ever gained by threatening the Japanese, their psychology being such that threats are likely to wholly prevent their exercise of correct judgment."

Only a very few changes have been made to Admiral Hart's narrative. Occasionally he misspelled a name; those errors have been corrected. In instances where he used only an officer's last name, all efforts have been made to provide that man's first name in parentheses. The meaning of some of the more difficult or obscure acronyms, so beloved by the military, have been provided parenthetically. And finally, Hart's 19th century tendency to capitalize every other noun has been scaled back to render the text more readable. Except for those minor edits, the narrative is precisely as the admiral wrote it.

This edition of Hart's wartime account begins with a biographical overview, the reading of which may help both the World War II novice and expert alike to more satisfactorily navigate the story that follows.

Charles Culbertson

Biography of Thomas C. Hart

Admiral Thomas Charles Hart – the last commander of the Asiatic Fleet – was born June 12, 1877, in Genesee County, Michigan, the son of Thomas Mansfield and Isabella Ramsey Hart. He attended public high schools in Davison and Flint, Michigan, prior to his appointment at the age of 15 to the U.S. Naval Academy in May 1893. While a naval cadet, he won the gold medal for rifle competition and for two years was coxswain of the academy's crew. Hart graduated 13th in a class of 47 on June 4, 1897, and served two years at sea – which was required by law before commissioning. He was commissioned ensign on July 1, 1899, and his subsequent promotions were as follows:

Lieutenant (junior grade) July 1, 1902; Lieutenant, August 16, 1903; Lieutenant Commander, July 1, 1909; Commander, August 29, 1916; Captain (temporary), February 1, 1918; and (permanent), February 7, 1921; Rear Admiral, October 1, 1929; and Admiral, July 25, 1939.

After graduation in June 1897, Hart joined the recruit training ship *Alliance*, in which he served until December of that year, when he was transferred to the *USS Massachusetts*. He served in that battleship during the Spanish-American War, participating in the Cuban campaign, and in the battle of Santiago on July 3, 1898, when Admiral Pasqual Cervera's Spanish fleet was destroyed.

During the remainder of 1898, Hart served in the yachts *Vixen* and *Hist* and on January 26, 1899, reported for duty in the battleship *Indiana*. In October of that year he was assigned to the training ship *Hartford*. From October 1902 until May 1904 he was an instructor in the department of ordnance and gunnery at the U.S. Naval Academy. He was then transferred to the battleship *Missouri*.

While an instructor at the academy, Hart met Caroline Brownson, daughter of Rear Admiral Willard H. Brownson, superintendent of the academy. He courted her and the couple were eventually married on March 30, 1910. They went on to have five children, three of whom served with the navy during World War II.

On December 9, 1905, Hart assumed command of the torpedo boat destroyer *Lawrence*, and served in this, his initial command, until that ship was decommissioned in November 1906. He then commissioned and commanded the *USS Hull* and served in that command until June 1907. The succeeding two years he was on duty in the navy department's bureau of ordinance in Washington, D.C. While serving in that assignment he had temporary additional duty as aide to the assistant secretary of the navy from January until June 1909.

Returning to sea, he served as ordnance officer of the *USS Virginia* until December 1909. After duty in connection with fitting out the *USS North Dakota*, he was assigned as gunnery officer in that battleship from her commissioning on April 11, 1909.

Hart reported in October 1911 for duty at the Naval Torpedo Station in Newport, Rhode Island, where he served until September 1914, when he joined the *USS Minnesota* as executive officer. Detached from that duty in February 1916, he assumed command of the Third Submarine Division, Pacific Torpedo Flotilla. In May 1917 he was ordered to the United States and in July was assigned to command the submarine base in New London, Connecticut, with additional duty in command of the *USS Chicago*, and as chief of staff to the commander of the Atlantic Fleet's submarine force.

In August 1917 he was transferred to command submarine divisions 4 and 5, Atlantic Fleet, in the submarine tender *Bushnell*. That group operated in European waters during World War I. In April 1918 he was given temporary additional duty at Queenstown, Ireland; London, Portsmouth and Harwich, England, and other places for visits and consultation with British authorities. In July 1918 he returned to the U.S. After temporary duty in the *USS Chicago*, Hart was assigned as director of submarines in the office of the chief of naval operations in Washington.

For service during World War I, he was awarded the Distinguished Service Medal with the following citation:

"For exceptionally meritorious service in a duty of great responsibility as Commanding Officer of two divisions of submarines. One sent to Ponta Delgada, Azores, and the other to Bantry Bay, Ireland, and establishing the submarine patrols and methods of operation. Also for distinguished service under the

Chief of Operations in the performance of duty in connection with submarines."

After the Armistice in November 1918, Hart continued to serve in the office of the chief of naval operations until July 1920. He was then ordered to command Submarine Flotilla 3, operating with the Asiatic Fleet, with additional duty in command of the submarine tender *Beaver*. From March until August 1921, he was also in command of Submarine Division 18. Returning to the U.S. in June 1922, he was under instruction at the Naval War College in Newport, and then at the Army War College in Washington; from June 1924 until May 1925 he was a member of the faculty of the latter college.

On June 6, 1925, Hart assumed command of the *USS Mississippi* at Honolulu in the Hawaiian islands, serving in that capacity for the next two years. In July 1927 he reported at the Third Naval District, New York, where he served briefly as assistant commandant and the supervisor of the New York Harbor. On October 4 of that year, he became inspector of ordnance in charge at the naval torpedo station in Newport.

Back at sea in 1929, Hart, while serving in the submarine tender *Holland*, was promoted to the rank of rear admiral. In 1931 he was appointed superintendent of the U.S. Naval Academy at Annapolis, Maryland, and served in that post until June 18, 1934. He then returned to sea as commander of the *USS Louisville*; between that time and 1936 he served as commander of Cruiser Division 5. He then became a member of the Navy Department's general board in Washington, and in December 1936 became chairman of the board.

In April 1939, Hart was designated commander in chief of the Asiatic Fleet, assuming command with the rank of admiral on July 25, 1939. Serving in that command prior to and following the outbreak of World War II, he displayed unusual abilities in handling the manifold problems confronting him.

After the attack on Pearl Harbor on December 7, 1941, the Japanese withdrew from the Central Pacific and for the time being, except for the capture of the islands of Wake and Guam, confined their major attacks to the Philippines Islands and the Netherlands East Indies (N.E.I.). American operations were of limited to that line of enemy advance. Guam was easily taken by the Japanese. The forces on Wake fought gallantly against overwhelming odds, and exacted a steep price for their eventual surrender to the Japanese at the end of December.

Except for the forces in the Philippines under General of the Army (then General) Douglas MacArthur, the American strength in the Western Pacific consisted chiefly of the Asiatic Fleet, a few aviation units, and the garrisons of Marines at Guam and Wake. The small Asiatic Fleet commanded by Admiral Hart included the heavy cruiser *Houston*, the light cruiser *Marblehead*, 13 overage destroyers, some 29 submarines, two squadrons of Catalinas comprising Patrol Wing Ten, and a few gunboats and auxiliaries which could not be counted on for combat. With this force (plus the light cruiser *Boise*, which happened to be in Asiatic waters when the war warning was received) they undertook to delay the enemy's advance until they could muster sufficient strength to put up any real resistance. There was no real hope of stopping the enemy campaign, but the effort made by Hart and the Asiatic Fleet nevertheless contributed materially to the ultimate check of the Japanese advance. It constitutes a remarkable chapter in the history of naval warfare.

During the latter part of November 1941, when Japanese advances along the coast of Indo-China indicated the approach of a crisis, Hart sent the *Marblehead* and eight destroyers to Borneo. Likewise, the *Houston*, *Boise*, and the destroyer tender *Black Hawk* had been dispatched to operate in southern waters. On the evening of December 8, after the Japanese had bombed U.S. airfields and destroyed many army planes, Allied submarines and motor torpedo boats, which were still in Philippine waters, were left with the task of impeding the enemy's advance. On December 10, the navy yard at Cavite, which had long been recognized as insecure, was practically wiped out in an air attack which also damaged the submarine *Sealion* and the destroyer *Peary*. On the same day the Japanese landed on the islands, after which all attempts to bring in effective quantities of supplies by sea proved unsuccessful.

At the close of 1941, Hart set up his headquarters in the N.E.I. Shortly thereafter General Sir Archibald P. Wavell of the British army assumed supreme command in that theater, whereupon

Hart became the commander of the Allied Naval Forces ABDA (American-British-Dutch-Australian). Up to this point, as far as the Asiatic Fleet was concerned, the campaign was conducted along plans worked out in the Navy Department prior to the outbreak of hostilities. In January 1942, the Japanese had overrun the Philippine Islands, and the greatest part of ABDA strength was in the N.E.I., for which the enemy was headed. Submarines and motor torpedo boats were engaged in slowing down the enemy advance to give Allied forces as much time as possible to get organize for the surface actions that were in prospect in the Java Sea.

In that situation, Hart had to plan all operations without air support, except for a few army bombers and a few fighters based on Java. The PBY4s of Patrol Wing Ten were unsuited for the operations; only the superb work of their pilots in the face of enemy fighters, coupled with the mobility of the tenders, made their use possible Collecting the few ships at his disposal, Hart decided upon a night torpedo attack. This was delivered off Balikpapan (the action became known as the battle of Makassar Strait) early in the morning of January 24, 1942, by the destroyers *John D. Ford*, *Parrot*, *Paul Jones* and *Pope*. The attack was successfully executed and was responsible for the stalling of that particular force for some time at Balikpapan. Hart's classic order to the Asiatic Fleet just before the battle of Makassar Strait was, "Submarines and surface ships will attack the enemy, and no vessel will leave the scene of action until it is sunk or all its ammunition exhausted."

Further seeking to delay the enemy drive, a striking force consisting of four cruisers and seven destroyers, about half of which were Netherlands and the other half American, was formed under the command of Rear Admiral Doorman of the Netherlands navy. Doorman tried to attack a large enemy convoy at Balikpapan, but his forces were discovered by Japanese planes. A prolonged bombing attack foiled the plan. During that attack, *Houston* suffered one direct hit which destroyed her number three turret and *Marblehead* was so damaged that she was forced to retire to the States. Continuing their advance, the Japanese attacked Palembang in southeast Sumatra and entered Banka Strait.

In a second effort to interfere with the enemy operation, Doorman was again forced to withdraw by enemy planes. By February 14, 1942, the Japanese in Borneo and Celebes were positioned to advance on Bali and Eastern Java, and Japanese forces in Sumatra also threatened Java. At this point in the campaign, in accordance with some agreements made in Washington and London, Hart relinquished operational command of Allied naval forces ABDA, to Vice Admiral Helfrich of the Netherlands navy.

Hart returned to the United States and in May 1942 President Franklin D. Roosevelt presented a Gold Star in lieu of a second Distinguished Service Medal to Hart for his service. The citation reads:

"For exceptionally meritorious service as Commander in Chief, United States Asiatic Fleet. In that position of great responsibility he exercised sound judgment and marked resourcefulness in dealing with the difficult military and diplomatic situation prevailing prior to December 7, 1941, and upon our entry into war with Japan disposed and handled the Asiatic Fleet in a manner which left nothing to be desired. His conduct of the operations of the Allied Naval Forces in the Southwest Pacific Area during January and February, 1942, was characterized by unfailing judgment and sound decision coupled with marked moral courage in the face of discouraging surroundings and complex associations."

The Asiatic Fleet ceased to exist as such in June 1942, and Hart was detached as its commander in chief on July 1 of that year. He was placed on the retired list of the U.S. Navy in the rank of admiral, in recognition of his "conspicuous and distinguished service in operations against the enemy in the Far East from December 7, 1941, until February 14, 1942."

Hart then served as chairman of the board of awards in Washington. In February 1944, the secretary of the navy detailed Hart to hear and record the testimony of navy personnel who had firsthand knowledge of the Japanese attack on Pearl Harbor. Because some of these naval officers were on dangerous assignments – assignments from which they couldn't leave and might not return – Hart went to them for their testimony. He returned to the United States from the

Pacific in April 1944, and continued duty on the general board of the U.S. Navy Department. On February 9, 1945 he was relieved of active duty so that he could accept Connecticut Governor Raymond Baldwin's appointment of him as senator from Connecticut. He was sworn in as the newest Republican senator from Connecticut on February 15, 1945. Congressional historians were unable to find any previous instance of a high-ranking regular naval officer becoming a senator.

When asked how he would react to the pressure groups in Washington, Hart's prompt answer was: "There are two strong words in the English language – yes and no."

In late 1945, after Germany and Japan had been defeated, Congress began an investigation of the December 7, 1941, attack on Pearl Harbor. One of the most useful pieces of evidence Congress would have at hand was the report written by Hart based on the interviews he had conducted with navy personnel in February 1944.

When his term in Congress expired, Hart chose to retire rather than seek election. He and his wife settled on the family farm in Sharon, Connecticut. Here, on this 265-acre farm which his wife's ancestors had farmed since 1790, Hart lived in quiet retirement until his death on July 4, 1971, at the age of 94.

Charles Culbertson

Admiral Thomas Charles Hart

Narrative of Events
By Admiral Thomas C. Hart

A background to any operational narrative for the Asiatic Fleet's preparation for war and of the events during the war's first two or three months needs to be supplied by outlining the steps which were taken toward joint operations with the N.E.I. (Netherlands East Indies) forces and the British forces – particularly the latter.

It can be properly begun about mid-January 1941, when Commander (John L.) McCrea came to Manila and acquainted us with the outlines of a new war plan. At the time of his visit, the chief of staff, Rear Admiral (William R.) Purnell (then captain), was at Singapore engaged in the second conference with the British (first one was 8-15 November 1940). Incidentally, Admiral Purnell attended all of the conferences, four in all, with the British and the Dutch, directly representing CinCAF (Commander-in-Chief of Allied Forces), and hence became the officer of that fleet who was best in touch with what would probably face us in case of a war with Japan while we were allied with the British and the Dutch.

The main lines of the cooperative position which our Asiatic Fleet occupied, vis-à-vis the British and the Dutch, were briefly as follows:

Under the first plan, which Commander McCrea brought out, the intention was that we would reinforce our Asiatic Fleet with at least a cruiser division, one carrier, and a squadron of destroyers, while the British navy would continue mainly engaged in the Atlantic – and perhaps the western part of the Indian Ocean. Later, February to April, 1941, the position became reversed in that our Asiatic Fleet was to receive no surface ship reinforcements, whereas the British fleet would be reinforced heavily, with battleships and carriers included. The question of unified command of naval forces never became at all definite. At first the trend was toward American command, and then later toward British command, corresponding to the relative preponderance of naval forces available. All through the negotiations and conferences the Dutch naval command occupied a position quite subordinate to the British; they tended to be in closer touch with the British command than were we, particularly so as

11

time went on and exchange of visits between Java and Singapore increased.

A characteristic of the aforesaid negotiations, conferences, etc., was that the British navy seemed always to primarily feature the control of trade routes over broad areas (with particular regard to ocean escort of the empire's troop and supply convoys), whereas we tended to minimize the requirements in that respect to the consequent availability of naval concentrations prepared for direct combat. Consequently, there was a rather basic conflict between British and American views; this not only obtained in the Far East, but is also understood to have existed in Washington – so there was no disagreement on this major point within our own service. One result was that, all through the period leading up to the war, there never was any agreement with the British (and Dutch), under which strategic control of the Asiatic Fleet was to pass out of American hands. Therefore, only "cooperative action" was provided for.

The British naval authorities at Singapore, with the Dutch participating, made considerable progress with joint war plans (known as PLENAPS), based upon the forces available but also useful if naval forces were considerably increased; they always supplied CinCAF with copies, one of which went to OpNav (Naval Operations). The British naval authorities were never able to obtain concrete commitments from either the Australian or New Zealand navies, both of which held out and retained the idea of concentrating their own ships in their home waters in case of a war with Japan.

As far as the Asiatic Fleet was concerned, the war began with no commitments toward the British or the Dutch except for one minor one: To supply the British Far Eastern Fleet with destroyers, up to two divisions, if and when that fleet grew to the intended dimensions, comprising capital ships, carriers, etc. We still were in the position of otherwise exercising complete strategic control of the Asiatic Fleet when the war began.

Looking back at this time, the lack of preparation for joint action between the three navies in that area was really seriously disadvantageous in only two particular factors – the personnel of the Asiatic Fleet had acquired no familiarity with the N.E.I. and Malayan waters and preparations for joint tactical operations were quite incomplete. There was also the lack of personal acquaintance as among officers of the three fleets; but the most disadvantageous circumstance was American lack of familiarity with the waters in which they later had to fight. Fortunately, however, considerable preparations had been made in the field of joint communications with the British and Dutch. As a result of two very comprehensive conferences on this subject, and with the benefit derived from a fairly lengthy practice period, in the use of the special cryptographic aids and radio channels, radio procedure, etc., the outbreak of war found us reasonably well prepared in the field of joint communications.

It will be recalled that Admiral Tom Phillips, R.N. (Royal Navy), arrived in Singapore with *Repulse* and *Prince of Wales* about 1 December 1941. The new British commander in chief came to Manila almost immediately (and before conferring with either the Australian or New Zealand navies, or with the Dutch commander in chief); he arrived there on 5 December. Before that time I felt that the situation had become such that there would be no objection in going to Singapore for conference myself, but Admiral Phillips moved first. We conferred through 6 December, with Lieutenant General (Douglas) MacArthur present until the conference became strictly naval and in detail (incomplete stenographic record is available). A joint despatch to the respective governments was agreed upon and sent, late on 6 December. Admiral Phillips then returned to Singapore (flying both ways) to follow up by conferences with the Dutch, the Australians and the New Zealanders, but the war came on before such conferences were held.

Note: Chief Air Marshal Sir Robert Brooke-Popham visited Manila early in April 1941 and once or twice subsequently. The first visit had no result and I doubt that the later ones did. There was a good deal of attendant publicity which I considered to be quite undesirable inasmuch as all the Allies still had much building-up remaining. It was not timely from the standpoint of international relations to forewarn enemies by such show of conferences. Those between navy officials were kept secret, whether held in Singapore, Batavia or Manila.

Events Up To 1 June 1941

Commander in chief, Asiatic Fleet, arrived Manila Bay 21 October 1940, and thenceforth none of the fleet was north of Philippine waters, with the exception of the China gunboats and the occasional scheduled visits of the navy transports. There had already been discontinuance of forwarding Marine replacements into China for the detachments at Tientsin and Pekin. This was later extended to the Fourth Marines at Shanghai, so that all the Marine detachments in China ran down in numbers, to the consequent increase of the Marines in the Philippines. Also, either *Tulsa* or *Asheville* were being kept in Philippine waters, leaving only one of those two vessels with the South China patrol.

Upon arrival in Manila, commander in chief soon found that the commandant of 16th Naval District was in unsatisfactory mental and nervous state and he dropped out from illness on 12 December. This entire period was characterized by personnel difficulties in the 16th Naval District which, indeed, endured to the end. After an interim of some weeks, during which the second-in-command of the district carried on, a third rear admiral arrived, about four weeks before the outbreak of the war. There were, therefore, in all, five officers who acted as commandant of the district within one year. This in itself was a source of inefficiency, at a time when the demands upon the district incident to increased work in serving the fleet, plus the handling of a good many "projects" in preparation for war, placed a heavier load upon the personnel of the district than had ever obtained before.

The naval establishment in Manila Bay was, of course, most inadequate and difficulties of an industrial nature were very great. Unfortunately, the best personnel obtainable, which in such a situation might have improved matters to a great extent, was not available. The department had for far too many years sent officers, line officers in particular, to the 16th District who were not of the quality that the conditions called for. Olongapo did run very well; its commander and the constructor (for the *Dewey*) were excellent.

This situation, which is very briefly sketched above, was always a handicap to the correct functioning of the Asiatic Fleet command as a while. Nevertheless, in upkeep of material, we were usually able to meet the most important demands and, since the naval facilities at Cavite and elsewhere in Manila Bay were mostly put out of action very early after the outbreak of war, these deficiencies did not constitute a serious handicap after hostilities actually began.

During the period, and subsequently, a mass of directives involving alterations to ships was received from the Navy Department. Most of them showed no differentiation over similar ships on other stations, some seemed not to fit Asiatic Fleet's own special requirements and the total involved was so great that available industrial facilities would have been swamped if it had all been taken on. In consequence, commander in chief established priorities to control the character and quality undertaken – of these alterations which have been ordered by the Navy Department. A number of them were of such low priority on that list that Cavite never even approached undertaking them.

The industrial force at Cavite became expanded to the limit of the plant. In order to better care for immediate needs and to increase potentialities for future Navy Yard work, various small plants in Manila were given contracts for work within their capacity which resulted in some alleviation of the congestion at Cavite. This practice did also set up sufficient organization for utilization of those commercial facilities.

During the period, in addition to various small 16th District "projects," looking toward better preparedness, there were underway three large ones: Extension of underground navy facilities on Corregidor, the section base at Mariveles and the naval air station at Sangley Point (Cavite).

The underground work, Corregidor, was instituted in the spring of 1940 and it was a vastly important project: Invulnerable radio communications, torpedo and ammunition storage and handling and storage for spare parts, general supplies and provisions. The work was done by the army, proceeded rather slowly and was still incomplete in November 1941. But the installations were of great use, nevertheless; for instance, essential radio communication was never interrupted for long, even under heavy bombardment.

The section base was started with very primitive construction facilities and went very slowly at first. It was well conceived and included storage and some maintenance facilities as well as those for operations. The work had gotten far enough along, by December 1941, for the establishment to be very useful, except for the net depot which never got started; such net planting as was accomplished was done with very primitive facilities. The construction of the ammunition depot, Mariveles, scarcely got started; the contractor had only just finished his usual rather elaborate living and working establishments for his own personnel.

The naval air station, Sangley Point, never even approached completion and, anyhow, it was mostly burned out by the first bombing attack. Of course it was in a location quite vulnerable from the air – and it was likewise so in conception and design. That base was a $5 million project, as conceived and designed under control of the Navy Department. The CinCAF had proposed a $2 million air station, which would have meant fewer eggs in one basket, but his principal argument was that the less elaborate – and semi-permanent – establishment could be completed earlier. However, it may be said here, but for general connection and as applying to all plane and preparations, that CinCAF had insisted upon a policy of concealment and dispersal within his own command, as an essential defensive measure. That policy had obtained from the winter of 1939-40 and it applied to the entire command.

There was set up (autumn of 1940) an auxiliary operating air base at Olongapo; it had been continuously occupied and used for many months before the war. Preparations had also been made for operating from Los Banos, on Laguna de Bay, where concealment of planes along the foreshores was somewhat practicable; the facilities there were extemporized and at practically no expenditures.

From the winter of 1939-40, the words AS-IS came to be applied to Asiatic Fleet war plans. This was because of insistence upon having in readiness operating plans which were based upon going to war with the forces and facilities which were actually in hand. There had been too great tendency to build plans around forces, etc., which had been recommended, requested, or only hoped for. Parenthetically, it may be mentioned that said tendency was fostered somewhat by the department's basic plans and its instructions for preparing contributing plans. As applying to the 16th District, those instructions complicated matters and the trend was toward too much theory. The time had arrived (1940) when plans had to be practical and with readiness to use what actually existed – apart from efforts to build up forces and facilities. The AS-IS policy increased the labor of planning because changes had to be made as reinforcements were received or as facilities increased. The format and the compliance in detail with the department's instructions probably was not good. Even with our shortcuts, the plans were usually not strictly correct or up to date but the AS-IS idea did pay when the time came.

During the period, there was close touch by CinCAF and by commandant, 16th Naval District, with the commanding general, Philippine department, Major General (George) Grunert, who was entirely cooperative and willing to come half-way. Despite that fact, little progress was made toward cooperative action between the arms where it was most needed – the respective air detachments. The main reason was that Army Air was building up rapidly, in fighters particularly, absorbing many partially trained pilots and was, in general, in such a preliminary state that cooperation seemed not yet timely. A brigadier arrived to take over the Army Air command but he soon went off on mission to China, Malaya, Java, etc., and his arrival did not promote cooperative arrangements.

In conjunction with the army, the plan for mining the entrance to Manila Bay was extensively revised. For years that plan had been defective in that extremely little attention had been given to navigating the entrance by our own shipping after the mine-fields were laid. (Under the old plan such navigation would have been so difficult and dangerous that egress and ingress would have been impracticable under most weather and visibility conditions). Furthermore, army's fields had previously been planned with no thought of enemy submarines. The plan for the army's mine-fields was extensively changed and navy's somewhat. Arrangements for moving the *Dewey* and for mooring her in operative condition at Mariveles were completed.

CinCAF also entered into a verbal agreement with General Grunert under which the mining of Manila Bay could be done <u>in</u>

part: army to plant either its inner or outer field – or both – and navy only to make a bluff at planting its mines; but we were to send out warning notices to the effect that all entrances were dangerous and to put into effect the regular arrangements for patrol and for taking shipping in and out through the gates. It was estimated that some time would elapse before it could be known that the Navy mine fields were a bluff and that we would get the effect of a full closure for a period. Then, mining turned out to be unnecessary, there would not be much loss because the army mine is recoverable; the navy mine, of course is not. Furthermore, planting the army fields was bound to be a long process whereas, when the time came the Navy fields were supposed to be planted very quickly. There was frequent consideration, over many months, as to whether or not the situation called for planting but this arrangement never was effected. Navy and War Departments eventually ordered all the fields planted.

During this period, commander in chief, Asiatic Fleet, was somewhat too often in a disadvantageous position because of untoward delays in obtaining necessary information from Washington. This was due, in part, to a lack of understanding of Far East conditions by subordinates in the Navy Department. The most prolific source of the difficulties lay in failures to transmit secret documents with necessary despatch.

This period was also marked by the beginning of publicity, including speeches, which were directly threatening against the Japanese. Commander in chief viewed this tendency with considerable alarm because nothing is ever gained by threatening the Japanese, their psychology being such that threats are likely to wholly prevent their exercise of correct judgment. Furthermore, such threats appearing in the press, etc., (though naturally most of it was from wholly unauthoritative sources), tended to put the Japanese too much on guard against the preparations for war which were then being made in the Far East or which shortly followed.

In late 1940, all naval dependents were sent from the entire station, including the Philippines; there were over 2,000 women and children. At Guam there was an additional 100 but, (reason unknown), they were not evacuated until late 1941. The army's dependents followed the navy's in a few months. Dependents of other federal officials in China were evacuated at the same time as the navy's but the same practice was not extended to such dependents in the Philippines. That was unfortunate.

The fleet, under the department's direction, took four Danish freighters into "protective custody." They were diesel ships; all deck officers and sufficient engineers to run them were found on board. A considerable effort was devoted toward retaining that personnel intact and in a proper mental attitude so that the ships could be readily put into operation when so directed.

There was established, in Manila, an enlisted men's club in a building constructed for the purpose by the commonwealth and used by us on a rental basis. This filled a long felt need in that it contributed greatly to the men's comfort and health and tended to reduce disciplinary offenses by liberty men.

The "Neutrality Patrols," which were established in the autumn of 1939, were continued through the period. But the administration of those patrols was such as to feature our own war training. The objective of such flights, moreover, became the Japanese rather than nationals of the participants in the European War.

The Asiatic Fleet based at Manila Bay from its arrival in the autumn of 1940 through the ensuing winter and carried on usual schedules of type exercises, etc. Also, there were inserted some periods of exercises which involved all types. There had been a dearth of such work because of the usual peacetime duties which had to be met on the Asiatic station.

The Asiatic Fleet submarines had been increased in number from six to a total of 17, without any increase in tender facilities. This is a condition which is not particularly disadvantageous unless extended over long periods. However, the shortage in tender facilities on that station did exist for a long time and was a source of privation for personnel, and of difficulties in maintenance. The fleet should have received another tender at the same time as the submarines, instead of being required to fit out a merchant ship, as a tender, on the station. There were even great delays in getting the ship, (the *Otus*), in hand and no very great progress was ever accomplished toward converting the ship into an adequate tender. One of the Danish freighters would have been fully as suitable as a tender and she lay in Manila from July, 1940. We made an effort to have her purchased for the purpose but the deal fell through, in Washington.

The greater part of the fleet spent about six weeks, April and May, 1941, in the southern is lands, (Tutu Bay, Tawi Tawi, etc.). Scheduled exercises were continued from those southern harbors over the period, and the fleet returned to Manila Bay at the end of May.

Looking forward to the possible loss of Manila Bay as a base for the fleet, we took the following measures: There was loaded into *Pecos, Trinity* and the large tenders as much spare ammunition, torpedoes, spare parts, general supplies and provisions as the ships could carry. This meant a considerable quantity, (2,500 tons), and though the conditions for storage, particularly as regards explosives, were reasonably safe they were not in accord with usual naval requirements. These measures still left good supplies of all such material in Manila Bay with the exception of certain machinery spares for the combatant surface ships. Not many submarine spares were included – only what *Canopus* could stow. It was all planned in detail, extended even to the spare propellers and some shafting and did generally put the fleet into much better position to meet serious eventualities than would otherwise have obtained. Additionally, about 150 of the largest aircraft bombs were put in charge of the British navy at Singapore through a quite unofficial arrangement, intended to conceal the fact. The auxiliaries consequently were loaded rather deeply and the two tankers had to be limited somewhat in their future cargo fuel capacity; this, however, was not great because in the good weather which usually prevailed, they could be safely loaded down below the usual marks.

From 1 June to 15 June 1941

Early in June, the commander in chief decided that the time had arrived to set up his command post on shore, where strategic command could be readily exercised and to thus place the fleet in a better condition of readiness for its initial deployment for war. The reasoning was briefly as follows:

The estimates of the situation as heard from Washington and as seen from our narrower field, but in closer proximity to Japan, had been in general concurrence. In November, 1940, CinCAF had submitted an appreciation which concluded that the Japanese intended further aggression and that such would most likely be to the southward. Later, during early spring, opinion changed – no signs of building up for a southern advance had become manifest – and the department was informed that we thought that a Japanese invasion of Siberia had become the more likely. That opinion prevailed for only a few weeks. During the spring it was seen that the Japanese were becoming more squeezed economically. They were not getting oil out of the N.E.I. at anywhere near the 1,800,000 tons per annum rate and were being more and more restricted in obtaining other raw materials, from the south the southwest, by the measures of our own government as well as by the British and Dutch. Parenthetically, the people of the United States seemed to have become more anti-Japanese than before and the press was indicating a sentiment against anything in the nature of appeasement. Since an inability to obtain replenishment of oil supplies would alone, and soon, mean a desperate condition for the Japanese the situation bade fair to become menacing.

By May, 1941, it had been settled that Asiatic Fleet would not be reinforced with surface ships but that there was intention to very heavily increase the British fleet in the Far East. The natural sequence would be that if a joint naval commander was established he would be British. The little joint planning which was being actually accomplished was between the British and Dutch local fleets – with an informal understanding that any of our naval forces which went south would expect to fit into their tactical plans. Our war plan for initial deployment placed our surface ships toward the south but the various considerations in the picture effectively prescribed that those ships should be under a task force commander; and also, apart from facility of radio communications, that the Asiatic Fleet administration and strategic command should be from on shore, Manila Bay. Authority for moving the fleet office ashore was obtained from the Navy Department.

Consideration was given to establishing the fleet command post at Cavite or Sangley Point, but that idea was discarded. Commander in chief's presence would have tended to interfere with the proper status and functioning of the offices of the 16th Naval District. All space and facilities there were already taxed and an added activity in that space would have been disadvantageous from all standpoints. Moreover, it was seen that it was most desirable for Commander in Chief to be located for easy and convenient conference with U.S. Army authorities, looking toward improved arrangements for cooperation. The same applied as regards the American high commissioner, but to lesser degree. Since, also the fleet anchorage was naturally near to Manila, for leave, liberty and supply purposes), it was decided to establish the shore command post in Manila City. There was no Army office space available to us and provision for a joint command post was still in the planning stage.

The most suitable place was in a building on the waterfront which the State Department was planning to use for the U.S. consul and the trade commissioner. An effort was made to obtain this space, but the state department was entirely non-cooperative and, though the needs of its officials were of quite minor importance and already fairly adequately looked after, the Foreign Service did not recede from its position.

Accordingly, some space was rented in another building, also on the waterfront. This space was sufficient and was suitable except that it was in a commercial office building where maintenance of secrecy and security of papers, etc., was difficult and required strong guards.

During the period there was disclosed other instances of important documents being badly delayed on the way to CinCAF from Navy Department. The difficulties seemed to lie in the great slowness and the mistakes in operating the system for transmission of secret mail. In the end, no real damage resulted but the repeated failures caused uneasiness, to say the least.

Received a personal letter from Vice Admiral (Geoffrey) Layton, R.N., indicating that his command now had authority over the British oil industry in northwest Borneo and would institute preparations for demolition. This was a sequence of considerable "conversation," briefly as follows:

During the winter of 1939-40, it became apparent within the Asiatic Fleet command that the Far East petroleum supplies constituted the one strategic raw material that would be absolutely vital to Japan in war. In late 1940, all of the high officials of the "Stanvac" Company, (whose holdings were mostly in Sumatra), were in Manila – following attendance during the N.E.I.-Japan conference on oil which had recently been completed in Batavia. CinCAF obtained from the Stanvac officials some up-to-date data concerning the industry and certain "inside" information on the general picture surrounding that situation. On all occasions thereafter – and particularly during Captain Purnell's various conferences at Singapore or Batavia – every opportunity was taken to urge upon such authorities as could be reached the necessity for readiness to deny the N.E.I. petroleum to an invading enemy. We represented that common knowledge to the effect that thorough preparation and resolution, to that end, existed would serve as a deterrent to the prospective enemy.

Naturally, the vast importance of the subject was apparent to all who would think about it and our prospective allies had it in mind all along. It was at the same time clear that commercial and business interests, and rivalries, were very much in the picture – hence our urging and even insistence about a readiness and a will for destruction. The order of good faith in which the various oil companies met the requests for said preparations seemed to be: (1) Stanvac (2) Dutch-Shell (3) the British company in northwest Borneo. The latter seemed to make little progress toward this "scorched earth" preparation until the British commander of the fleet required authority.

16 June to 30 June 1941

The Russo-German war began and it was definitely a surprise for we had received no indication that the Russians would not grant a sufficient number of the "requests" which we had heard the Germans were making on them. This event caused CinCAF to again consider the probability of a Japanese aggression into Siberia rather than to the south. There was indication that the German attack on Russia was also a surprise to the Japanese, which was naturally a factor in the picture.

All things considered, it seemed likely that the Japanese would direct any new aggression into the channel that seemed most profitable to them, irrespective of what the rest of the Axis wanted. Therefore, a southern advance still seemed likely and, whichever way things turned, it was seen that our own plans should primarily be on that basis. Consequently, we made no change in either our plans or in our mental attitudes.

During the period, word was received from the Navy Department that Washington had withheld approval to the report of the last Singapore conference, as not meeting the purposes of the prospective allies in the Far East theater. Incidentally, that last conference had really ended only at about the point at which it should have begun and had not produced a practical, realistic plan which would carry through. There were so many conferees present that difficulties were great, without prior agreements, agenda, etc., and it was too hard a task for the presiding officer to handle.

However, there was not much cloudiness as regards the Asiatic Fleet's situation and what was expected of it. There was agreement and understanding with the Navy Department on the general lines of a war plan involving the Far East. It was clear that the initial deployment of surface combat ships and of large auxiliaries was to be to the southwest, most probably to base on Singapore, but the department continued to leave much to the discretion and initiative of CinCAF. In his hands remained the decision as to what ships would deploy to points outside the Philippines and what ships, if any, were to pass to the strategic direction of any other commander.

At the end of the period, the fleet offices were established in the Marsman Building, on the Manila Harbor waterfront. A task force was established with the chief of staff (Purnell) commanding, and assisted by an operations staff only. All files, documents and fleet flag equipment which would not be needed by the task force commander were moved off *Houston* – into storage or to the fleet office. Henceforth, all fleet administration and all operations of units not included in the task force (which became designated Task Force Five) were from on shore.

No extra officers, other than some V-7 ensigns for coding boards, were taken in, for fleet or task force staffs. That meant harder work for the staff officers but their working conditions became improved; *Houston* had been very crowded and hot. The fleet office was continuously open, with watches established as on board ship. Radio communications were established in the fleet offices; there was also a visual signal watch, with adequate equipment, so that rapid communications were as good as when the fleet flag was ship-borne. As soon as these arrangements were completed, the Asiatic Fleet command was streamlined for war. There would remain, at most, only the transfer to *Houston* of less than one patrol plane load of administrative staff personnel with equipment. The fleet office eventually became quite adequate and satisfactory. Its establishment and its work would have required much less effort if it could have been in the Tourist Bureau Building, in the space which the State Department insisted on having for its consul.

During the period, the fleet held a goodly number of those gunnery exercises which require the most in the way of equipment and services. The fleet's work was somewhat interrupted by typhoons.

1 to 15 July 1941

The *Asheville* was totally disabled off Swatow, China, during bad weather. *Marblehead* was sent to the rescue and towed this gunboat to Manila; she as well as *Tulsa* was henceforth retained in Philippine waters. The *Marblehead* again showed high efficiency in that mission; she was an old ship but her personnel always made the best of what they had and this cruiser could always be depended upon.

The Task Force, (the surface ships, including large auxiliaries, and also the submarines), left Manila Bay and operated in the southern waters. The harbors of the Sulu chain were most used but the ships visited other ports as well. Task Force Five commander's directive was to return ships, in small detachments, to Manila Bay for two- to three- day visits, in order to replenish stores as needed and to give liberty. The two tankers continued their rather frequent voyages to N.E.I. oil ports for cargo. The fleet had for some time been getting most of its fuel from those fields and it was obtained from at least three ports in order to work up latitude and elasticity in supply. We began administration toward keeping all navy-owned tankage filled and also began working on the commercial fuel companies to the end that they would keep as heavy reserves as possible – particularly in Manila tanks.

From this time onward, three to six patrol planes operated continuously along the southern boundary of the Philippines. These operations were in part neutrality patrols and in part for general security. Later, an unofficial understanding was entered into with the Dutch navy under which there was some linking up with the air patrol which they had long maintained along the northeast boundary of the N.E.I. The patrol planes based on their tenders. Certain minor basing facilities were also extemporized on shore on Balabac Island and in the Gulf of Davao.

A damaged British battleship passed through bound for Bremerton. This was the second British man-of-war to visit Manila for fuel, etc., while bound to a U.S. port. We made every endeavor toward secrecy and avoidance of publicity but the British personnel showed no great interest to that end.

In an excellent public speech, on 4 July, the American high commissioner, the Honorable Mr. (Francis B.) Sayre, showed a decided change in mental attitude toward the possibilities in the international situation. A few months previously he had thought that the possibility of our becoming involved in a war in the Far East was quite remote.

Editor's Note:
At this point in Admiral Hart's narrative, a missing page truncated his narrative for the period July 1-15 and foreshortened his report for the period July 16-August 14, 1941. However, it is clear from the narrative as it continued after the missing page that he was discussing the mining of the harbor at Subic Bay. The narrative continues with that theme.

The warning notices were issued repeatedly but keeping ships out of danger consumed much effort; all small craft available were assigned to the duty and even destroyers had to be used occasionally. There was loss of one or two small vessels and some lives despite all precautions.

The plan was to defer laying the mine field at Subic Bay and the outer navy field off the north Manila Bay entrance until the dry-dock *Dewey* was moved. The dock arrived at Mariveles on 22 July and was there moored in condition for docking ships; she was made self-operating and self-sustaining

Much material and several tools, as well as personnel sufficient for operations, were brought down from Olongapo. Conditions were difficult and the many obstacles to operations were overcome by efficient and devoted effort of the personnel. Lieutenant C.J. Weschler was in charge and was both untiring and very able. The *Dewey* later accomplished a great deal of ship work at Mariveles and continued in operations even after the siege of Bataan was well along. By the end of this period, Olongapo was abandoned except as an auxiliary air base and for occupancy by Marines and some navy personnel.

Two weeks elapsed after the department's order before CinCAF was able to report to Washington that Subic and Manila Bays were closed by mines; and the fields were far from complete even then. It was previously known that the army's planting would be slow, but the Navy's was expected to be rapid. One reason for the slowness did lay in adverse weather for it was the season of the year's worst weather along the west coast of Luzon. Moreover, it was somewhat evident that the type of mine supplied the navy was so delicate in certain features that very highly specialized personnel was required. The naval district either did not have the requisite personnel available or did not properly administrate it because the mining went badly. In addition to technical errors, there was also deficient seamanship and poor arrangements for handling the planters. The fleet gunnery officer and the personnel of two, (Bird), sweepers which had recently arrived on the station, eventually solved the technical and the planting difficulties. But so many mines were lost that the integrity of the fields was considerably depreciated.

During the period, we heard that current opinion in some quarters was to the effect that the Japanese would attack Siberia, but we made no modification in our own preparations or attitude. CinCAF informally called the department's attention to the vulnerability of the Marines and gunboats which were in China. He also advised, informally, that another flag officer be sent to command the naval district so that the industrial activities could be separated from the district command. (This was before the current commandant was invalided).

The operations of Task Force Five continued as before. Its commander was in Manila for two days – in *Houston* which had returned for supplies. It was entirely apparent that the task force and its training were being efficiently handled.

15 to 31 August 1941

The period was uneventful as far as the Asiatic Fleet was concerned. It included the completion of understandings on certain points in war plans – which were not of major importance. CinCAF prepared an "appreciation" concerning the continued retention of his forces in China which set forth his opinion that they should be withdrawn to the Philippines in the near future. An election of commonwealth officials was pending and was the subject of greatest current interest within the Philippines.

1 to 15 September 1941

This period also was unmarked by events or decisions of any considerable importance. The large projects looking toward larger scale readiness of the naval district began moving along at a better rate. Cavite continued routine work on ships. The task force continued its training in southern waters with ships returning to Manila every four to five weeks, in detachments. Because of the very great shortage of submarine tenders, the six S-class submarines being based at Manila as well as was possible. The first of the Pacific Fleet cruisers which had begun to escort important west-bound ships arrived. Many more American and British officials than usual were stopping off at Manila as they travelled on their various missions.

Little information concerning the Japanese was being received from any source. Such news as did arrive indicated that the financial and economic measures which had been effected against them were resulting in such pressure that the Japanese would have to effect adjustment in the not far distant future.

The press indicated that there was a rather widespread belief in the States that the tension in the Far East was becoming eased. More authoritative advices did not agree and while there seemed hope that there would be a peaceful settlement of the outstanding difficulties with the Japanese, there was no definite ground for optimism. However, the Japanese fleet was found to be returning to home bases and there was no evidence of increasing occupation of Indo-China.

The *Henderson* made a routine transport voyage, including calls at China ports. No replacements were sent to our forces in China and there were some withdrawals additional to short-timers, so that the remaining forces were: At Pekin and Tientsin, 200 Marines and navy. At Shanghai, 800 Marines and Navy. Also three gunboats on the lower Yangtze and one in South China. The Navy Department had rejected the recommendation that those forces be withdrawn concurrently with this voyage of the transport. CinCAF had, aside from his concern about personnel in the vulnerable locations, hoped to obtain the commander of the Yangtze patrol for other duty. Another flag officer was badly needed in the Philippines.

Information received indicated that strong army reinforcements were arriving in the Philippines, or en route, and that about 80 modern pursuit planes were already on hand. There occurred, (23rd), a protracted interview between the commanding general USAFFE (U.S. Army Forces in the Far East) and the CinCAF, at the latter's instance. It was learned that the USAFFE was going far beyond the war plans, by including in the defense zone virtually all of the Philippines except Mindanao and Palawan. The plan envisaged a fully equipped ground army of 200,000 (eleven divisions) and a powerful air detachment. The date of complete readiness was to be about six months in the future. CinCAF put forward the necessity for cooperation, generally, but more specifically as between army and navy aircraft. He also made known to the commanding general the major points in all the conversations with the British and Dutch fleets and explained our current situation as regards joint action with those forces.

The rear admiral commanding 16th Naval District was invalided home. There were continued instances of failure to receive important information from the Navy Department, and CinCAF was constrained to make an official protest. The fuel situation was improving in that increased stocks of boiler and diesel fuel were being kept on hand. The situation was less satisfactory as regards high-test gasoline. All fuel storage was vulnerable from the air. Much of the navy's gasoline was in drums which were kept dispersed as much as practicable.

The fleet received six modern motor torpedo boats which were transported on the deck of the *Guadalupe*. Such transport required extensive deck fittings and, while so fitted, it is to be regretted that the ship was not employed to carry out another half squadron of the PT boats. We had expressed the belief that the Philippine waters would be the most favorable location possible for that type of weapon. Was informed that another submarine reinforcement, for the Asiatic Fleet, was under consideration. The CinCAF emphatically urged that an adequate submarine tender accompany, or precede, any reinforcing submarines. He also urged upon the department that an additional patrol plane squadron be despatched to the Philippines. It was also strongly recommended that a full squadron of navy dive bombers be sent out, forthwith, for reconnaissance purposes in the dangerous Formosa sector as well as for their offensive power. We had a tentative promise of availability of army aerodromes in north Luzon.

1 to 15 October 1941

The numerous visits of high officials during this period continued and included Dutch army officers. Air Chief Marshal Sir Robert Brook-Popham also came to Manila, from Singapore, for a second visit – ostensibly for conferences on Army affairs. There was considerable attendant publicity, to which the air chief marshal was not adverse, and CinCAF advised the Navy Department that such was an undesirable feature; that in view of our vast defense preparations, in hand but far from complete, time was in our favor and that noting unessential should be done to precipitate matters. CinCAF conferred very briefly with Sir Robert – there seemed to be little to talk over.

CinCAF conferred with the commanding general, UFFE, and informed him of the current and prospective dispositions of the fleet an on the reinforcements which had arrived, or were pending. The subject of aircraft cooperation over the sea was also discussed and CinCAF stated that he would produce an official letter which would set forth his own proposals and serve as a concrete basis for further discussion.

Task Force Five returned to Manila and was temporarily inactivated, the command and staff moving to the fleet office but leaving all in readiness for re-activation of the task organization and command. The ships had been away from base, for the most part, over a period of three months and needed to return for more supplies and various other attention. Such information as was available indicated that although the situation vis-a-vis Japan remained tense, there was not great immediate danger of a rupture and that the time was as favorable for the ships' return as would likely be afforded. Another important matter for port attention concerned the loads of munitions and material in the large auxiliaries. The conditions of storage had been unfavorable for four months and some rehandling of it was required. Furthermore, a good deal of fleet administration was in arrears and required the presence in port of ships, unit commanders, and full fleet staff. The CinCAF also had in mind discussions of broad scope and the possible reconsideration of the fleet's operating plan.

The departure of the task force from Manila was not scheduled during the period. The southern Philippine harbors were open to submarine attack, whereas there had been provided at least some minefield protection in Manila Bay. We were not at the time in position for the use of harbors in the N.E.I. or Malaya. There was no 100 percent solution which would give security against surprise attack.

16 to 31 October 1941

During the period, the underground work on Corregidor and the building-up of the section base at Mariveles made good progress. The fleet's work in harbor continued and some underway exercises were held. Two destroyers collided during night exercises and were thereby disabled for several weeks (*Peary* and *Pillsbury*). Information was received that *Holland* and 12 large submarines were being transferred from the Pacific to the Asiatic Fleet. CinCAF wrote a formal letter to commanding general, USAFFE, as a basis for more concrete understandings concerning air operations over the water.

The Japanese cabinet underwent a reorganization. The news of it was reason for concern and new decisions as regards added security precautions. We established an off-shore air patrol over about 100 miles of the west Luzon coast, with particular coverage for exercise areas, and also set an anti-submarine sound patrol by destroyers. Much consideration was given toward return of the cruisers, destroyers and large auxiliaries to more southern waters and CinCAF decided against that step. A far reaching proposal was under study at the time and:

On 27 October, CinCAF proposed to the Navy Department that an initial deployment of any ships to the south and west be abandoned as a basic part of the war plan; and that, instead, the fleet plan to fight the war with all ships based on Manila Bay. The considerations were:

No real progress had been made toward agreement on joint naval operations with the British and Dutch and there were no commitments except our promise to supply some destroyers when the British fleet acquired capital ships.

There was some question as to the effectiveness of operations, under the circumstances, as based along the Malay Barrier.

Assuming reasonable harbor security, the fleet could be more effectively employed from Manila Bay, on account of its strategic location; also surface ships, submarines and patrol planes would be, severally, more effective when handled in conjunction with each other.

34

Lastly, and collaterally, all U.S. forces would be definitely employed in defending the Philippines – or in conducting offensive operations from there. (There was little said about this particular consideration, which was largely psychologic).

The fleet command and staff was by no means unified and in agreement on the correctness of that proposal of 27 October. There was much argument which hinged, of course, on the real situation as regards the probably security and integrity of Manila Bay as a naval base. The proponents argued that the situation had already greatly changed by the building up of the USAFFE which would very soon be strong enough to withstand a heavy amphibious expedition; and that although an enemy would probably get his bombers through at times, the U.S. Army pursuit squadrons had become so strong that there would be no sustained bombing attacks on Manila Bay. The opponents argued that USAFFE would not be built up into sufficient strength for some months; and that while pursuit planes were available in considerable numbers (said to be 100 plus), there would not therein be sufficient opposition to provide anything like the security that we needed. The opponents of the proposal were headed by the chief of staff. He was right.

1 to 15 November 1941

The period was somewhat marked by uncertainty and indecision. As heretofore recorded, CinCAF had previously felt a lack of timely information from the Navy Department and grave delays had been experienced in the transmission of what was sent. In those earlier instances no disadvantage resulted which was of considerable importance. Although request for decision on the important despatch of 27 October was made on 6 November, no reply had been received by the end of this period and that circumstance was quite disadvantageous. Some despatches, particularly one received about 12 November, contained the department's instructions on comparatively minor matters and unfortunately the CinC thought there was contained certain indication that his proposal to fight the campaign from Manila Bay with the entire fleet was meeting some favor. No definite steps were thereupon taken toward implementing that proposal but, on the other hand, the detailed preparations for an initial deployment to the southward were not pressed; certain munitions, supplies, etc. were not hurried back into the large auxiliaries. The combatant ships were maintained in sufficient readiness (normal maintenance continued), but such was not altogether the case with the auxiliaries; the extreme congestion of Cavite's waterfront made handling stores a slow matter, which added to the seriousness of losing time.

The war plans officer from Singapore, Captain (John A.) Collins, R.A.N., and our observer there, Captain (John H.) Creighton, U.S.N., were in Manila 2 to 3 November. The CinCAF informed them concerning the broad lines of his proposal of 27 October. The subject of loaning destroyers for operations with British capital ships was also discussed as a separate issue. The department had been informed that under certain circumstances such loan up to two divisions could be made.

The effort at entering into adequate arrangements for joint operations of army and navy aircraft, over the seas, met with a decided rebuff from the USAFFE. Toward the end of the period, some disposition developed toward meeting us but there seemed to be unwillingness to go as far even as the arrangements which for some time had been in effect in the Hawaiian Islands; and no great progress was ever made in the Philippines toward unified air operations. During the period, PatWing Ten photographed Spratley and Itu Aba Islands. Little development was found on Spratley but considerable was discovered on the other island.

A few sets of radar equipment arrived for the USAFFE and one set was received for the Marines, which was put at the disposal of the army. It was unfortunate that this highly important equipment did not arrive sooner, and in greater quantity, so that an adequate air-warning system could have been in full being. The CinCAF, with commanding general, Philippine department concurring, had urged early in the year that a few Navy sets be sent out and set up at appropriate locations on shore. No defense equipment was more important.

The section base, Mariveles, progressed more rapidly and arrived at the point of some utility. We began assembling provisions and general supplies in its storehouses. There was some progress in laying the torpedo baffle nets across Mariveles entrance; the planting methods employed were very primitive. We completed plans for improving the security of that anchorage, as against submarine entry, with mines. Also began placing permanent moorings – buoys and dolphins – to increase the berthing capacity of the enclosed space.

Eight large submarines arrived from Pearl Harbor on 8 November and brought word that *Holland* and the remaining four submarines were starting later; also that the squadron commander, who was slated to take command of all the Asiatic submarines, would arrive with the last detachment. Heavy cruisers were calling with greater frequency as ocean escorts of transports from Hawaii.

The CinC received the department's directive to withdraw Marines and gunboats from China. Since the N.E. monsoon was now at its height, the voyage of the river gunboats was foreseen to be a feat of seamanship. Decided that, in any case, we would get the Marines out of Shanghai ahead of the gunboats but they immediately began assembling. Two (American) President liners were chartered for earliest possible despatch to Shanghai, where the Marines would be able to load at short notice. Those at Pekin and

Tientsin had to proceed to Chinwangtao for embarkation and their movement to that port was likely to be slow. (The withdrawal order was received embarrassingly late).

Mr. Kurusu passed through Manila, en route to Washington, and CinCAF saw him at a reception given in his honor. The conversation was brief; Kurusu remarked that his "mission was to keep our Asiatic Fleet idle" but he evinced no real hopefulness of succeeding in whatever his mission really was.

The Philippine election was completed, permitting some abeyance of politics. Most of the travel by the clipper was being under "prior preference" controlled at Washington. Many writers were traveling in that category. Officer messengers coming straight by plane from that city and bringing the latest information could have been very helpful at this time.

16 to 30 November 1941

There was definite information during the period that the Japanese army was engaged in considerable movement along the China and Indo-China coasts. Those movements could be estimated as presaging only increased occupation of southern Indo-China or of an advance into Thailand; a few held opinions to that effect.

There was no definite information of Japanese naval movements that carried much significance. The fleet staff was busy during the first few days of the period in revising the operating plan on the basis of fighting a campaign from Manila Bay with all the fleet – less any forces loaned to the British fleet. No further information or instructions on that point having been received from the department, the CinCAF on 18 November informed a full conference of unit commanders concerning the proposals which he had submitted and stated that, although approval had not been received, time did hot permit further delay in definitely undertaking the corresponding preparations.

The department's despatch definitely withholding approval was received on 20 November. The department's estimate and instructions were correct and the proposals of CinCAF, 27 October, were wrong. No harm would have ensued if CinCAF had not been allowed to persist in his error over a vital period of three weeks. As things eventuated, the damage was not so very great anyhow and perhaps was offset by the fact that the fleet did "stand-by" the USAFFE more persistently than a cold-blooded estimate of the real situation called for (If there is benefit therein it is of course psychologic only).

Upon receipt of the department's despatch, all plans and preparations were immediately thrown back upon the original basis – with initial deployment of surface forces to be to the southward. (As before mentioned, the inadequacies of facilities ashore slowed up changes in the loading of auxiliaries, etc.) The CinCAF did, however, decide to retain all submarine tenders in Manila Bay. That turned out to be an incorrect decision. The 29 submarines themselves constituted most of the potentiality of the fleet; they could be most effective if they operated with the strategic advantage of Manila's location and they needed all the services which the tenders could supply if the boats were to retain their effectiveness over any considerable period. Therefore, as seen at the time, risk had to be taken.

Since the availability of ComYangPat, (Commander, Yangtze Patrol, Rear Admiral William A. Glassford) could by then be foreseen, it was decided to put him in command of Task Force Five, upon his arrival. The CinCAF adhered to his decision of June 1941, to maintain his own command post in Manila and also decided to directly command the coastal frontier – which had far outgrown its original dimensions and by then comprised the greater part of the Philippine waters. Only the original sea defensive zones, in and off Manila and Subic Bays, were kept under Commandant 16's jurisdiction and only enough surface craft or that coverage was permanently assigned to the district; however, the small ships were switched back and forth between fleet and district as the day-to-day demands called for. In consequence of these arrangements, the CinC retained personal command of submarines, the patrol wing, the motor torpedo boats and some of the small surface craft which were to operate within the sea frontier. A larger staff was therefore required than had been contemplated in June. Rear Admirals Glassford and (Francis W.) Rockwell were both "new" in the duties which were to confront them. Rear Admiral Purnell was fully experienced and was variously in demand; the CinCAF decided that he must be retained for the duties of chief of staff. Preparations for a joint army and navy, (including air), command post had been underway for months. It was being constructed by the army, underground at Camp McKinley, which was not an advantageous location for the navy but the army considered the underground spaces at Corregidor unsuitable on account of the location. However, the preparations at McKinley were months from completion and that installation never got into the picture.

During the period, we began moving explosives out of the casemates of the naval magazine, Cavite, and placing them in a large ammunition dump established in the open along a beach a few miles from Cavite. The greater part of such inflammables as paints, dryers, etc., also was moved out of Cavite. The large quantity of filled gasoline drums was further dispersed; by this time we had gasoline widely scattered about in the Manila and Subic Bay areas as well as small caches at various outlying points. The CinCAF directed that certain projects for elaborate bomb-proof structures be discontinued and that available effort be directed toward extensive provision of bomb shelters giving reasonable security against fragments and blast but not against direct bomb hits.

On 24 November, CinCAF sent *Black Hawk* and four destroyers to Balikpapan; *Marblehead* and four destroyers to Tarakan. Those were the two east Borneo oil ports; the detachment commanders' instructions were to go to them for fuel but to "have difficulty" in obtaining full loads – with a view to occupying the ports, or vicinity, for a protracted period if necessary. *Houston* was directed to further hasten the completion of mounting four 1.1 inch quadruple machine guns, then to proceed to Iloilo or vicinity and await the arrival of commander, Task Force Five.

The CinCAF received, on 26 November, a Navy Department despatch which indicated very serious developments in the American-Japanese relations. The American high commissioner received a similar despatch on the following day and, in consequence, called into conference the commanding general, USAFFE, and the CinCAF. All three conferees set forth the current situation as concerned the activities and responsibilities in their own fields, and discussed any additional measures which seemed possible. One of the three expressed greater optimism than did the other two; all were fully aware of the necessity for promoting an optimistic spirit in the lower echelons.

The *Holland* and four submarines arrived. The two squadron organizations were inactivated, washing out that command and administrative echelon so that the chain of command was direct from commander submarines to the division commanders. The latter, five in number, assumed staff duties in addition to their nominal command functions – which latter were not to be exercised at sea except under circumstances calling for special orders to that effect. The division commanders were specialized in their staff capacities – two for operations, etc. One squadron commander took over duties as chief of staff to commander submarines and was especially charged with operations and training. The other squadron commander had the department's orders as commander submarines and the date for turn-over was set as of 1 December. When the turn-over actually occurred, the outgoing officer – Captain (John E.) Wilkes – was held at Manila for eventualities. The commander of destroyers was informed that a war would be a division commanders' war and that it was unlikely that he would command destroyer formations at sea.

The two President liners loaded the Fourth Marines, and attached naval personnel, at Shanghai, with the greater portion of their movable equipment and supplies and sailed, separately. Four large submarines had been sent to escort them from a point to the northward of Formosa. Of the three Yangtze gunboats, the smallest was laid up at Shanghai, pretty well stripped down and equipped for demolition; (when the time came, the personnel failed to destroy her). The other two then sailed for Manila; *Pigeon* and *Finch* were sent north to escort the gunboats down because there was no experience to show the effect of rough water on them; the "Bird-Boats" themselves got into trouble on account of the bad weather on the way north. The South China gunboat, *Mindanao*, was held at Hong Kong until the developments with the other two were known. Inasmuch as it had previously been represented that she could be useful in defending Hong Kong it was unwise to subject her to too much weather risk.

Toward the end of the period, a valuable army convoy was nearing Manila, under escort of *Boise*. The *Langley* was just arriving to replenish stores and revise cargo, having been held in the southern islands for a long period, tending the air patrols and establishing two extemporized air bases. *Trinity* and *Pecos* were arriving with full loads of fuel which they had taken on in the N.E.I.

On 29 November, received a definite war warning from the Navy Department. Additional to the disposition of ships previously listed, in the foregoing, the forces of the fleet were occupying the following stations 29-30 November:

Three destroyers were on listening and general patrol off the Manila-Subic Bay entrances. The remaining two of the squadron were still at Navy Yard, repairing collision damages.

Three submarines were in Navy Yard hands. The remainder were in Manila Bay or were training in the vicinity. The three submarine tenders were scattered from Mariveles to Manila Harbor. The practice of berthing submarines alongside tenders in large numbers, or in large "trots," had been discontinued. No more than two were being alongside or together and all berthing was considerably dispersed.

There was one aircraft detachment based on Balabac and one in Davao Gulf. Each comprised one small tender with patrol planes in the eastern detachment and utility planes at Balabac. The planes were patrolling off-shore and linking up in an informal arrangement with the Dutch planes. One full squadron of PBY's was basing on Sangley Point, the remainder of the large planes at Olongapo; in each case a certain degree of localized dispersal and concealment was being practiced. An auxiliary and extemporized base at Los Banos, (in Laguna de Bai), was ready for use.

The remaining small craft were in Manila Bay or vicinity. The inshore patrol and guarding of the mine fields continued to absorb much effort of small craft; and more of them than was usual were in Navy Yard hands.

1 to 7 December 1941

The Marines arrived from Shanghai and were disembarked into Olongapo, via tugs and lighters, with weapons, munitions, field equipment and all supplies. The Fourth Marines immediately set about reorganizing as a 3-battalion regiment, equalizing the strength from the 600 to 700   Marines of the battalion that was already in the Philippines, etc. The regiment was told to occupy the Bataan Peninsula for the present, from Mariveles to Olongapo and somewhat to the northward of the latter. Having mostly long service men and a full complement of regular officers, the Marines were the strongest infantry regiment in the Philippines; it was not equipped for rapid movement.

One of the President line ships was turned around as quickly as possible and sailed for Chinwangtao to embark the remaining Marines. She never arrived there. The army convoy arrived on the 4th; its escort, *Boise*, was fueled and supplied and sailed for Cebuto to await further orders. The *Mindanao* sailed from Hong Kong about 3 December and arrived at Manila on the 9th, having encountered considerable difficulty with the N.E. monsoon seas.

The two gunboats from Shanghai had less difficulty and, with the two "Bird Boats," arrived at Manila on the 4th; all three river gunboats joined the inshore patrol. Rear Admiral Glassford set about getting in touch with the situation and at constituting a staff preparatory to assuming command of Task Force Five. It was regrettable that he could not have started such preparation some time before. Actually he reached Manila at virtually the last minute and at a time when all activity was particularly intense.

Langley, *Trinity* and *Pecos* arrived and prepared for departure. Tankage on shore was nearly full and there was difficulty in disposing of the cargoes of the two tankers. None of those three large auxiliaries had left Manila by the end of the period. *Isabel* was despatched to an outpost patrol station off the Indo-China coast. A small sailing yacht with auxiliary power was taken over and fitted out for a similar mission but the preparations were only just completed by 7 December. (This vessel was eventually sailed to Java and then to Australia by fleet personnel, including the flag lieutenant, who were evacuating to the southward).

The CinCAF, the commanding general of USAFFE and certain of their subordinates held a conference, on 1 December, on joint operations of aircraft over the seas. Preparatory conferences had been held by the air commanders and progress resulted on this date. It was agreed that Army heavy bombers would take over the patrol of the two northern sectors which touched Formosa. Their speed and ceiling better fitted them for coping with any enemy fighters that might come out from the Formosan landing fields. We obtained no enemy information from those planes during the period.

The navy patrol planes made a considerable number of long reconnaissance flights during the period. Those which went to the Indo-China coast were not routine flights but were at the personal, day-to-day, direction of CinCAF. The instructions were to avoid being sighted from the coast, or by Japanese ships, if practicable. The PBYs were sighted and at times by Japanese planes but they were not attacked. The patrol planes did sight a large number of transport and cargo ships in harbor or at sea. In Kamrahn Bay alone there were over 20 large or medium sized ships – with an air patrol over them – and numerous small craft. Not much enemy information was received, during the period, from other than the fleet's own sources. But it became very clear that strong Japanese amphibious expeditions were prepared to move.

Admiral Tom Phillips, R.N., the new CinC of the British Far Eastern Fleet, visited Manila, for conference on 5 and 6 December. This was at his own initiative and he had arranged to make the journey by air prior to his arrival at Singapore. Inasmuch as the conditions and circumstances which had previously prevented a visit by CinCAF to Singapore no longer existed, Admiral Hart would have proceeded to that port for the conference if the British authorities had given the necessary information. Admiral Phillips left Singapore prior to any meeting with Dutch or Australian naval authorities. The CinCAF proposed to him that Admiral (Conrad) Helfrich be included in the conference at Manila but the despatch got lost somewhere at the British end.

Admiral Phillips arrived at noon, 5 December, and departed during the evening or the following day; his presence in Manila was a carefully guarded secret. The afternoon and evening of the fifth was taken up with informal conversations which were followed by a somewhat formal conference that lasted well through the following day. The commanding general of USAFFE and his chief of staff were present during all the periods that involved other than naval subjects. During the conversations, CinCAF learned for the first time that the British had been assured of American armed support in any of four contingencies having to do with Japanese aggression against Thailand, the N.E.I., etc. It should be said that Admiral Phillips showed himself to be a remarkably able officer, possessing very broad knowledge, with keen intuition and judgment. Even though our association with him was brief we sensed that he was the best man that we had encountered.

Admiral Phillips was made acquainted with the general naval and military situation as for the Philippines, and he set forth the British situation and prospects. He had brought out *Prince of Wales* and *Repulse* and had just sailed the latter to Port Darwin – largely for political considerations. Additional British battleships were promised at rate which would have built up the capital ship force in the Far East quite rapidly. Admiral Phillips however did not have in sight a commensurate force of destroyers or of carriers.

During the discussions it appeared that, as yet, there had been no decided change in the British naval attitude in that protection of their sea supply routes as well as of the troop convoys was still primary. There was still the trend toward dispersal of forces. However, the new high command was obviously seeking combat and a coming offensive attitude was clearly seen. The immediate British naval concern was lack of destroyers; four had accompanied their heavy ships to the Far East but more were wanted at once. Consequently, Admiral Phillips requested the immediate loan of the two destroyer divisions which had been eventually promised. There was considerable argument between the two CinCs, on various subjects, but the main point of differences hinged upon that disposition of destroyers:

The CinCAF declined to send his destroyers to Singapore immediately. He represented that the British had only two capital ships in hand and had four destroyers with them; that there were two or three other British destroyers assigned to the local defense of Hong Kong which were the approximate equal of the American destroyers and which were currently not assigned to very good advantage; that the American cruisers needed destroyers for their full effectiveness and that the results from our large force of submarines could be promoted by the association of a few destroyers with them; finally, that though the promise for loan of American destroyers would be kept – and we had disposed them somewhat to that end – the time had not arrived to give up two-thirds of them.

Toward the end of 6 December, joint despatches were drawn up in the conference and sent to London and Washington. While the smooth copies were being made, word came from Singapore that a Jap amphibious expedition had been sighted in the Gulf of Siam, heading westward; there was a suggestion that its objective was an anchorage in Thailand. Admiral Phillips immediately recalled *Repulse* and said that if he were in Singapore he would go to sea with such ships as he could collect. Arrangements were made to send him in an American PBY if his own plane should, for any reason, be unable to make a night flight; he started for Singapore during the evening.

PatWing Ten's patrol flights did not go close in on the Indo-China coast on 6 December and did not see any expeditions on the move. As soon as the British information of the enemy in the Gulf of Siam was received, *Black Hawk* and one destroyer division were directed to sail from Balikpapan to Batavia "for supplies and liberty." That order started them to the westward and while en route the destroyers were directed to proceed toward Singapore and placed under the orders of the British CinC. Admiral Phillips was so informed as he was departing, by the CinCAF, with a remark to the effect that the differences as disclosed by the day's arguments were rapidly disappearing if still existent.

Japanese paratroopers attack the Dutch East Indies.

8 to 10 December 1941

Received notification of the attack on Pearl Harbor slightly after 3:00 a.m. (L.M.T.), 8 December. Informed the GHQ of the USAFFE and the Asiatic Fleet – with a directive to the latter to "govern yourselves accordingly." Recalled *Isabel*. The first landing on the Malay Peninsula occurred at about the same hour but we did not hear of it for some hours. The first attack on the Philippines was at day-break, by air, upon two PBY planes on the water at Malalag in Davao Gulf; those two planes were destroyed – the other two had taken off for patrol. The *Preston*, anchored at Kalalag, saw four enemy destroyers pass, steaming toward Davao, slipped out astern of them and escaped. At about 10:30 a.m., we received word that enemy planes were in the vicinity of Baguio. Later in the day we learned that enemy planes had made powerful and well executed attacks on U.S. Army landing fields in north central Luzon at midday, and had destroyed numerous planes as well as severely damaging the ground installations.

The respects in which the Asiatic Fleet was caught unprepared – additional to incomplete shore and harbor installations – has been set forth in the foregoing. The fleet made a good recovery. Rear Admiral Glassford and staff left for Iloilo by plane during forenoon of 8 December, to hoist his flag in *Houston* as Commander Task Force Five. His orders were to rendezvous *Houston* and *Boise* with *Langley*, *Trinity* and *Pecos,* which latter ships left the bay soon after dark that evening, screened by two destroyers; the destroyers eventually returned. While crossing the Sulu Sea, bound for Makassar Strait, the detachment encountered one enemy light cruiser, probably carrying a flag and screened by destroyers. Our ships drove them off and they were lost in the darkness. It is probable that this was a fortunate encounter in that the enemy estimated that our forces were likely to be encountered in that general locality in strength too great for the forces which he had available for fighting them. Anyhow, no enemy forces were met by the long string of merchant and other ships which were running south toward and through the Makassar Strait for several days afterward. Commander Task Force Five proceeded into Makassar Strait, assembling his forces and obtaining full loads of fuel at the Dutch oil ports.

The submarines sailed for patrol stations as per plan: One-third off enemy harbors; one-third stationed for intercepting enemy expeditions advancing on Luzon; one-third in reserve stations which were somewhat scattered and concealed. The submarines which were sent on directly offensive missions arrived after the enemy shipping had, for the most part, moved out and found only poor hunting for some time. They probably would have been more effective if they had been partly armed with ground mines instead of torpedoes only. The mines had only recently arrived and BuOrd (Bureau of Ordnance) had informed us that a defect had to be corrected before they were to be used. The submarines in reserve stations soon began to be fed into the defensive-intercept patrol lines, as the Japanese amphibious offensive developed against Luzon.

On 9 December CinCAF decided to restore the relieved commander of submarines, (Captain Wilkes) to that command on account of his experience and familiarity with the conditions obtaining – and his excellent ability, including health. It was also decided to send the thus displaced submarine commander south in *Otus* to have ready an alternative command post for submarines. On the following day, it was decided to also send *Holland* south with *Otus* – which meant the realization of the mistake of attempting to use all the tenders for servicing submarines in Manila Bay for a protracted period.

The air patrol obtained no information on enemy ship movements during the 8th and 9th. From this time onward an extraordinary crop of incorrect enemy information flowed in over the warning net. Too many reports came in of enemy sightings when nothing actually was sighted and when a vessel really was seen she was usually reported in one of two categories; irrespective of size, she was either a transport or a battleship! We received word of the capture of the Wake at Shanghai and of the surrender of the 200 Marines in North China.

The Naval Station, Cavite, was destroyed at noon, 10 December by Japanese bombers which bombed with deliberation, from above the range of the nine 3-inch 50 guns that we had installed for its protection. The enemy attack was not interfered with by our army pursuit planes and the bombing was very accurate. The damage was mostly from fire which effectively burned out the entire establishment, less the aircraft shops. Also, the fire was kept away from the naval magazine which still contained propellants and a small quantity high explosive.

The *Otus* was alongside a Cavite wharf loading torpedoes, spare parts and some equipment which had recently arrived for her own conversion. The ship got away, during the attack, with only slight damage but most of the material to be loaded was lost; it was only a small portion of the total available. *Peary* was completing repair of collision damages; she got away with minor damage but several personnel casualties. One sweeper was disabled, mainly through loss of machinery parts which were in the shops. The most serious loss was one of the large submarines which received two direct hits which entirely disabled her; she was later stripped of considerable gear and then fully wrecked with explosives. The other of the two submarines, at Cavite, received minor damages which were later made good by the tenders. The two submarines were just completing some of the numerous alterations which were on order.

The attack of 10 December made it entirely clear that, as far as security of ships and installations in Manila Bay was concerned, the enemy had control of the air. The *Holland, Otus, Isabel* and two destroyers were sailed that evening, for the south. Another, (9-knot), detachment consisting of *Tulsa, Asheville* and two sweepers also sailed; all to join Task Force Five. It is unfortunate that two or three additional small ships were not sent south at this time. Those two detachments also encountered no enemy on their voyages to the Borneo oil ports.

11 to 15 December 1941

During the attack of 10 December, a few bombs were dropped among the merchant ships just outside Manila Harbor. One medium sized ship was burned and sunk thereby. An extraordinary number of ships had fled for refuge in harbors and collected in Manila Bay.; Most of the small inter-island ships had come into the bay which also contained about 40 deep-sea ships of various ownerships; there were no very large ships but there were many medium sized ships that were valuable, some with valuable cargoes.

On 11 December, CinCAF called a conference of masters, owners and agents and advised as follows:

(a) That the inter-island ships were likely to be as safe while in ports or on voyages in the central portion of the islands and might as well work there; that they could thus in some measure assist the USAFFE's effort.

(b) That the deep-sea ships would eventually be destroyed if they remained in Manila Bay and that there was a fair chance of escape if they sailed to the southward. The fleet could not at once undertake direct convoy or escort, but was in position to cover, that some of its own ships had sailed the preceding night and that no enemy ships were being found to the southward.

The CinC's advice was accepted and ships began departing that evening. The movement continued for several days, with ships going out singly just after nightfall. All are believed to have escaped except one which was burned by a minor air attack. We were lucky.

It had been apparent for some days that our Pacific fleet could make no westward movement in force. The loss of *Prince of Wales* and *Repulse* and indications that the British defense of Malaya was not going too well gave little ground for hope in that direction also – as far as any diversionary effect on the enemy was concerned. Clearly the U.S. forces in the Far Eastern theater were on their own and the chance of getting reinforcements into the Philippines via the Torres Strait was not favorable. The mission of our naval forces remaining in or near the Philippines remained as before –

to support the USAFFE's defense while damaging the enemy as much as possible. He was already meeting success in landing forces in southeast and north Luzon. On 13 December advised the Navy Department that the situation of Luzon was very serious.

The air patrol discovered enemy men-of-war off north and northwest Luzon on 11 December and a half squadron of PBY's attacked a ship of the *Haruna* class, which was accompanied by cruisers and destroyers. It was a good attack, coming in from astern, made through thick anti-aircraft fire, but unfortunately, the salvo was dropped a fraction of a second too soon and the hits made were on the extreme stern. The attack at least disabled the enemy's steering gear and the damage may have been quite extensive. This was the last body of enemy combat ships that was found at sea by our air patrols.

On the following day Patwing Ten's luck was bad: A half squadron took off from Olongapo, on unjustifiably bad information, to attack "a battleship" nearby. The planes found nothing, were seen by enemy fighters which were not themselves seen and which attacked after ours had landed; seven PBY's were burned by incendiary bullets, two enemy planes being shot down in their attack.

By 13 December, our army planes were no longer keeping the air except for one or two fighters, at a time, flying for reconnaissance purposes. We then had a little less than one squadron of patrol planes operable and with little prospect of gaining further results commensurate with losses. The CinCAF therefore directed, (14 December), that ComPatWing (commander, patrol wing) Ten proceed to N.E.I., waters with remaining planes, all three small tenders and such extra personnel and remaining spares as could be carried. The voyage was made successfully and the tenders were ready to service a reinforcing squadron of PBY's when it arrived, in January, via a southern route to Darwin. After this movement south, there remained in the vicinity of Manila some damaged planes from which four were eventually made operable.

By the end of the period, we had withdrawn our four destroyers from Singapore and so much of the entire fleet had gone into Task Force Five that more staff assistance was there required. Therefore the chief of staff and six key officers in operations, communications and maintenance, were transferred to ComTaskFor Five. Admiral Hart decided to remain at Manila as long as the submarines could be operated and serviced from there. The chief of staff and one communications officer, carrying a letter of introduction, proceeded by plane, the others in one destroyer and the submarine which was damaged when Cavite was destroyed. There then remained in or based on Manila Bay:

Two destroyers.- one still repairing.
Six motor torpedo boats.
Twenty-seven submarines
Canopus and *Pigeon*
Three river gunboats.
Three sweepers and one fleet tug.
Various district small craft.

Nearly all the submarines were patrolling or in advanced stand-by stations and when they were in Manila it was only for short periods. With the destruction of Cavite, we were thrown back on *Canopus* for all services to submarines. In the interest of facilitating her work and of reducing damages from future bombing, *Canopus* was moored at the Manila Harbor front, in shoal water, and covered with camouflage nets. The torpedoes, spare parts, supplies and stores were moved into dumps – dispersed among the freight sheds in the vicinity. The submarine command post was established in the nearby Men's Club which also took on a large task of berthing and subsistence; some provision for bomb shelter was accomplished. This was the best that could be done for the submarines under the conditions of menacing air attack and it was hoped that the set-up could last for some time.

A few hide-outs were arranged – against the breakwater, among junks, lighters, etc. – which it was hoped the submarines could occupy without discovery while resting. The efforts at concealment were probably ineffective in view of the activity of enemy photographic planes – which seemed to hover about at will – and quite possibly our dispositions were being radioed from on shore anyhow.

The motor torpedo boats had arrived with experienced and trained personnel but the news of their addition to the fleet and information about their requirements had not been received in time to arrange for their basing or to lay down the outlying fuel caches which their short radius called for. Arrangements for basing them at Cavite had gotten fairly well along but it was all ruined on 10 December. Consequently, the employment of the PTs for combat had been thrown back, even if the enemy had come within their reach. They continued preparations for combat; (actually some use had to be made of them for messenger service between Manila and Mariveles, over several days). At the end of the period, the PTs – backed by one of the two available destroyers – were stationed to cover against a night advance of the enemy toward the Batangas-Tabayas wharves and beaches.

The three Philippine motor torpedo boats, which according to plan were to operate with ours, did not join up with them or report to Com 16. Those three boats never accomplished anything in operations involving combat. The American boats were highly successful during the later stages of the campaign.

Japanese bombing of the Philippines.

16 to 20 December 1941

The enemy's invading expeditions in northwest and southeast Luzon continued to advance and became well established. The submarines operated against them thickly, particularly in the vicinity of their landing points, and did damage but evidently not enough to disrupt the enemy's effort.

The naval district was doing its best at recovery from the bombing of Cavite. As many of the industrial personnel as could be used were shifted to the various small plants in Manila and progress was made toward carrying on supplying and repair work. The district commandant established a command post on Sangley Point and controlled operations from there. On 19 December, that area in turn received an accurate, high-altitude bombing attack which burned much of the gasoline that remained there in drums and ruined the radio installations – the latter by direct hits of large bombs. The naval hospital, which directly adjoined, was not touched; it had been abandoned because of its location, in the midst of military objectives. Com 16 then moved his command post to the prepared underground position on Corregidor. Cavite and Sangley Point were thereupon virtually abandoned except for handling salvaged supplies and making the preparations for complete demolition.

Two French merchant ships had been taken into "protective custody" somewhat earlier. During this period, one of them, an old-type freighter, loaded with a considerable quantity of flour and other provisions was sent to Mariveles to unload. She was bombed and burned, somewhat later, before the provisions were fully discharged. The other one, the *Marechal Joffre*, was a modern and valuable and, since she could not be "protected" in Manila Bay it was decided to try to get her away. About 100 navy personnel were thrown aboard and she sailed for Makassar Strait the same evening, being one of the last merchant ships to escape; she eventually proceeded to an east Australian port. The commander was a young lieutenant who must have done extremely well to surmount the difficulties encountered.

21 to 25 December 1941

The Japanese expeditions had been getting on very well with their invasion of Luzon. The enemy force in southeastern Luzon seemed to have a subsidiary mission but it had been making steady progress to the northward. The expedition on the northwest coast seemed the more dangerous one and it was coming down the coast fairly rapidly. It was clear that the enemy was doing a good job, that he understood amphibious war, could employ its natural advantages and could overcome its difficulties, including the coordinated use of all the varieties of forces and weapons needed. It is to be noted that in the entire campaign in the northern half of Luzon, the Japanese landings were on open beaches and their transports were never dependent on wharves. The enemy's ground equipment could not have been heavy and it probably was not elaborate.

Early in the period it became likely that the enemy would soon attempt landings in or near the Lingayen Gulf. That would be most dangerous to our defense and submarines were concentrated in that area – and its approaches – without regard to individual patrol stations. The instructions were to get at the enemy without thought of neighboring submarines which also might be attacking. Nevertheless the submarines again did not succeed in disrupting the enemy at sea. The best chance was in one incident off Cape Bolinao where one large submarine found herself in front of a convoy of large ships, with strong anti-submarine screen, in the late afternoon. She got off a contact report but did not succeed in attacking as the enemy passed – or by running in from astern that night. Next morning a considerable number of medium or large ships were at anchor in shoal water on the south side of Lingayen Gulf, and with a mine field to the seaward. They were attacked and probably damaged. In that difficult task, one S-boat touched off a mine or two and was hunted and depth-charged for over 24 hours. She barely escaped but had no serious injuries.

There had been conversations with the USAFFE concerning the employment of the Marine regiment but resulting in no definite arrangements or understanding. On 20 December the CinCAF made mention of the subject in a formal letter and subsequent staff conferences resulted in the following arrangement:

58

That the Marines, plus a naval battalion which was forming, would be brigaded with a regiment of constabulary, under a Marine brigade commander. The constabulary regiment was composed of fairly well experienced men but lacked good officers and non-coms which the Fourth Marines would supply from its wealth of experienced personnel. There was never time to carry out the project; the Marine regiment, as such, passed under the direct control of USAFFE and was mainly employed on Corregidor.

On 23 December, the CinCAF saw a copy of a USAFFE despatch which predicted an early retirement of all army forces to the Bataan Peninsula and Corregidor. On the following morning he received definite information that such movement was in progress, that the government and the GHQ of USAFFE would move to Corregidor that day and that Manila was to be proclaimed an open city, containing no combat elements. This eventuality had been foreseen but its coming so soon was a surprise – as was the fact that no mention of such a step had previously been made formally or otherwise, since the war began. We immediately proceeded to uproot *Canopus* and the other submarine installations from the Manila Harbor front and to shift all such activities to Tuariveles and Corregidor.

It was decided, in a full conference, that the submarines would continue to operate from Manila Bay and keep it up as long as possible. It was hard to decide whether CinCAF should also shift his command post to Corregidor or accept the probability that even the submarines would have to shift base to the southward in the near future – and make one jump of it to the N.E.I. The latter alternative was chosen. We had three patrol planes hidden in the mangrove off Los Banos, available for transport; also one submarine which had by then "worked up" after a main battery renewal. It was planned to send out one plane on the evening of the 24th, with the acting chief of staff and seven other commissioned and enlisted staff. (At the last minute, we gave up half the places to the top-ranking Army Air officers). We planned to sail the remaining two planes the following evening and also the submarine, carrying a load of personnel and the heavy communication equipment, files, etc.

During the forenoon of 25 December, the CinCAF turned over to Com 16 full command of all naval activities remaining in the Philippines, with a formal letter of instructions. This became effective at noon that day whereupon CinCAF's command post and radio station in Manila discontinued to function. The CinCAF had intended to take off after sunset on 25 December with 15 others in two PBY's and to make a night flight to Soerabaya, thereby being out of action for less than 24 hours. Unfortunately, the enemy discovered the two planes and burned them up in their hide-outs in the late afternoon. Consequently, only the submarine, (*Shark*) was available for transport; she left the Bay at 2:06 a.m. on 26 December.

26 to 31 December 1941

The *Shark's* voyage to Soerabaya occupied the period and was uneventful. Com 16 directed the two destroyers which had been left in Manila Bay to proceed south, on the night of 27 December. A little later he also directed commander submarines to shift his command post south and to discontinue attempting to carry out normal service to submarines from Manila Bay. It had become too late to get *Canopus* and *Pigeon* south. The ships were old and not of great value but the personnel was highly valuable. They did serve usefully in contributing to the defense of Bataan, etc., during the remaining months.

As indicated in the foregoing, the submarines did not succeed in disrupting the enemy's invasion of Luzon, even though two-thirds of them were employed on the task. Those results were disappointing to all concerned including the submarine personnel themselves. The personnel was long-service and experienced in peace-time training but – like everyone else – were not experienced in the kind of war that they faced; only war proves what is correct and what is wrong, who is effective and who is not. It can also be said:

That our peacetime training was not realistic in certain respects.

• That we also had not been realistic as regards the material which was too complex in installations that did not contribute directly to offense, or defense, and was lacking somewhat in the absolute essentials.

• That the enemy's mastery of amphibious war, by virtue of which he. could land most anywhere made interception of his expeditions very difficult.

• That the enemy employed large numbers of small ships, difficult to hit and that there was scant return when they were hit.

• That the enemy employed large numbers of anti-submarine craft; they seemed to be good at detection but not at attack, though it required time to learn that the hundreds of depth charges which they dropped were not very dangerous.

• That the last stage of the voyage of their invading expeditions was always at night – and during the dark of the moon at the critical periods. The enemy being in full control of the air, the submarines could be given no information of his ship movements approaching Luzon.

During the period, Task Force Five completed its assembly, fueling, etc., and moved the auxiliaries for occupation of Port Darwin as a main base. Its command completed organization, set up a command post at Soerabaya and held preliminary conferences with appropriate Dutch authorities. The merchant shipping by this time had all escaped, mostly via Makassar Strait.

Peary sailed for the south via Molucca Strait and there experienced considerable air attack; she was undamaged by the enemy attack but had some casualties from an attack by Australian dive-bombers from Ambon. *Heron* went north to assist *Peary* and was herself severely attacked; she held the advantage in the engagement, however.

By the end of the period the enemy was establishing at Jolo and at Davao for a further advance. Our submarines were tending toward a more southern theater, for their patrols, and opposing the enemy at those points. The damaged submarine, *Sealion*, had been repaired and sent on patrol.

31 December 1941 to 6 January 1942

Commander in chief, Asiatic Fleet, arrived at Soerabaya, Java, during the evening of 1 January and found the command post of Task Force Five established in the outskirts of the city in buildings which had been commandeered and supplied by the Dutch navy. The accommodations were sufficient and the post satisfactory except that radio facilities were inadequate. The fleet personnel did splendidly in extemporizing a main radio, from apparatus obtained locally and some taken out of ships, but the difficulties in handling the radio load were very great.

By this date Navy Department and War Department had fixed upon Port Darwin as a potential base of considerable magnitude and the trend was toward demands upon the place which its very poor facilities could not meet. Following the movement and also because security from enemy attack was at the time better there than at Soerabaya, ComTaskFor Five had sent all naval auxiliaries to Darwin. These voyages and also the escort of army and other shipping using the Torres Strait route employed cruiser and destroyers to such an extent that their center of gravity was, at the time, well to the eastward. The department was informed of the deficiencies of Darwin as a port and was also advised that the Torres Strait route might become too dangerous for our convoys at an early date.

There were ample fuel supplies at Soerabaya and at Darwin and all of our ships, including tankers, had filled to capacity at Balikpapan on the way south. The Dutch had made their base facilities at Soerabaya available and were accommodating in all respects. Those facilities were considerable but the base was congested and quite vulnerable from the air. All spares, munitions and special supplies were at Darwin a long distance away.

It was found that all ships of the fleet which were sent south had reached the waters of N.E.I. without much damage. *Peary* and *Heron* were air-bombed, during the period, in the Molucca Strait and both had some personnel casualties. In the case of the *Heron*, the action was protracted; the ship did splendidly, destroying one large enemy seaplane.

All but one of the numerous merchant ships which went south from Manila Bay had reached N.E.I. waters and were being managed by their own agents as regards disposing of and receiving cargoes. It was fortunate that the enemy had not been able to intercept this shipping; the aggregate value was great.

The Japanese had established themselves at Davao and at Jolo, from which points they later invaded the N.E.I. Patwing Ten sent six PBY patrol planes to make a daybreak bombing attack on shipping while the enemy was still in the building-up phase at Jolo. The section found the enemy off the north side of the Island but were intercepted by fighters and lost four planes; luckily, about 65 percent of the personnel were saved. Japanese submarines had appeared as far south as the Java Sea and were thereafter present most of the time for the remainder of the campaign.

We were informed that the enemy had completed his occupancy of Manila City. From the end of December onward, very little further information and practically no reports were received from Com 16 and the subsequent history of that area is not included herein. A considerable force of small craft had been left in Manila Bay under Com 16's command; by this time it became clear to CinCAF that he should have sent three or four more of them south before, say, 18 December including two of the sweepers. Similarly, too many officers and men of the navy were left in Manila Bay; 400 to 500 others might well have been brought out while it was still possible, even if risky; they were experienced and could have been more profitably employed in theaters other than Manila Bay. This error of judgment probably came from the idea of not going too far in withdrawing the navy from the defense of the Philippines. From Java things looked different!

On 2 January, received a despatch from OpNav which indicated some disappointment in the amount of damage which Asiatic Fleet had inflicted on the enemy. Also a despatch from Cominch (Commander in Chief), the last of which stated that the fleets would soon be placed under a joint command. CinCAF proceeded to Batavia on evening of 3 January and returned the following night. Purpose was to call on the governor-general and to confer with Vice Admiral Helfrich, commanding the N.E.I. Navy.

The Honorable Mr. (Hubertus J.) van Nook and Vice Admiral Helfrich were present at the interview with the governor-general. His Excellency stated that if the Japanese proposed that the N.E.I. withdraw from the war, and resume commercial relations, their proposal would be denied. The governor-general then proceeded to read a press report announcing the agreement to set up (British) General (Archibald) Wavell as a supreme commander, with GHQ on Java, Admiral Hart to command the three fleets, etc. He pressed Admiral Hart to set forth his basic ideas on the forthcoming campaign; he was told that the news came as a surprise that considerable thought and interview with General Wavell would be required first, etc. His Excellency then presented his own views, clearly, concisely and showing excellent knowledge and understanding of broad strategy and of the character of war which confronted us. His most cogent idea was that the campaign would be one in which the importance of ships and of aircraft would transcend everything else.

There was considerable time for interviews with Admiral Helfrich, the American consul general and others. It appeared to be the sentiment among the Dutch that the American reputation was badly damaged as a result of the events of the war in the Philippines. The Dutch navy was particularly cocky, principally because two of its submarines had each sunk four enemy ships in the South China Sea. Their attitude modified when *Seawolf* arrived at Soerabaya, (7 January), and likewise brought in a bag of four enemy ships which she had sunk off Hainan.

The Dutch navy had lost three submarines and the remainder was mostly in port resting and overhauling. The Dutch cruisers and destroyers were being employed as covering forces for Singapore convoys, and in A/S escort of their own shipping. Vice Admiral Helfrich had already provided space for a U.S. command post at Batavia, next door to his own, and strongly urged that we move into it and away from Soerabaya. He informed us that Admiral (Edwin T.) Layton was also preparing space at Batavia for a similar shift of the British Fleet's command post from Singapore, Admiral Helfrich was told that we were not likely to move because our fleet's operations would probably continue to be in the central and eastern part of the theater – hence Soerabaya would be the better location; anyhow it now appeared that the new supreme command GHQ would be in or near Batavia – and it would control.

Upon return to Soerabaya, CinCAF requested information from Navy Department concerning any prospective reinforcement of his fleet and any likely offensive movement by Pacific Fleet. This information was to be in preparation for the forthcoming conference with the supreme commander; it was not received.

Admiral Hart, lacking any instructions on the point, assumed that he would continue to command his own forces and proceeded to set up the Soerabaya command post to that end. It seemed necessary to have one of the two rear admirals at sea, to command a striking force, and arrangements were immediately made to re-embark Rear Admiral Glassford in *Houston*, with an adequate staff. The fleet command was to be exercised through, (and somewhat by), the chief of staff, Rear Admiral Purnell, who was fully informed and indoctrinated and who, also, was the American officer who by experience was best informed concerning the N.E.I. area and all matters pertaining to the Allied fleets.

It may well be said at this point that the Asiatic Fleet staff was a highly efficient and very adequate organization. It was mainly composed of officers who had enjoyed no previous staff experience. They had been together for a long time, had encountered many unusual conditions, had shown that they could rise to occasions and could always function efficiently despite poor working conditions.

At the end of the period we definitely learned that the British-Far East Fleet command post had vacated Singapore; that a post was being occupied at Batavia by a junior admiral who would command the three D-class cruisers, few destroyers and lesser craft which now composed that fleet; and that Admiral Layton would soon proceed to Colombo with most of the fleet staff and there await heavy reinforcements, including capital ships. A Rear Admiral, R.N., (Ernest J. Spooner), was remaining in command of H.M. dockyard at Singapore and would command sweepers and small local craft.

The commander submarines arrived from Manila, with staff, and set up his command post within the fleet offices. Captain Wilkes reported that the Japanese aircraft had become so active over Manila Bay and over such of the basing facilities as remained at Corregidor and Mariveles that it had been impossible to service submarines there any longer. Therefore he had been obliged to shift his base to the southward. It was not possible to bring out *Canopus* or *Pigeon*, of the submarine command. Also, a considerable amount of spare parts and torpedoes had consequently been left behind. Most of the torpedoes and some of the spare parts were brought out later, in submarines, but it was a mistake not to have brought out the two ships when it could have been accomplished.

Patrol Wing Ten also set up its command post at Soerabaya where it functioned for the remainder of the campaign under one of the squadron commanders – the two senior officers of the wing were taken into the supreme commander's H.Q. during the period. The wing's duties henceforth were altogether reconnaissance, which was mainly over the central and eastern part of N.E.I. waters.

The patrol planes were basing over wide areas, making full use of the three small tenders, and hence were difficult for the enemy to locate and destroy on the water. By this time, what remained of the wing had become highly experienced and efficient; the pilots contrived to maintain reconnaissance in the face of strong enemy air forces – by virtue of their skill in using cloud cover and ability in air combat, even against fighters. We had extra crews for which we began overtures toward obtaining some new PBYs which the Dutch navy had bought but for which they had no trained personnel. After considerable controversy, five of them were obtained.

During the period we completed new operating plans, reconstituted the cruisers and destroyers as a task force, (Rear Admiral Glassford), and organized a base command at Port Darwin, (Captain Walter E. Doyle). The cruisers and destroyers continued some escort and convoy work but were also assembling for covering the Makassar and Molucca Straits. The submarines were continuing to shift their patrol areas to the southward, to work against the

January 10, 1942. Left to right: Rear Admiral William Purnell, Admiral Thomas C. Hart, Lt. Gen. George Brett and Maj. Gen. Lewis Brereton

advancing enemy, but were also on his communication lines and of as many of his Indo-China ports as their numbers would permit. The submarines' results were improving but still there were occurring too many failures from torpedo defects and other causes. CinCAF was continuing to receive despatches over various routes, about getting ammunition, etc., into Corregidor. Army authorities were trying to collect enough to load a submarine – 20 tons.

On 9 January, Admiral Hart arrived at Batavia and thenceforth was able to visit the fleet offices at Soerabaya, or his ships, only for brief periods. He interviewed Mr. Elliot, of the Stanvac Co., and obtained late information concerning the oil industry and its situation, generally, as applying to the entire area, and particularly to the Palembang area. Mr. Elliot possessed an entirely correct war psychology and is very able. Through him we began fostering a commission to handle all the oil situation. Also Admiral Hart conferred with Lieutenant General (George A.) Brett and Major General (Lewis H.) Brereton, and stated his views as regards ship-

and-aircraft cooperation to which they expressed no disagreement. General Brett was not optimistic about holding the Malay Barrier and pointed out that Burma and Australia were the vital points – in his estimation – and that perhaps Burma could be held.

Admiral Layton had arrived from Singapore and there was a long conference between him, Admiral Helfrich and Admiral Hart. It was found that the British naval interests and activities were entirely centered on guarding troop convoys into Singapore; they were using the few small ships of their local command as well as the cruisers of adjacent commands which came into the area as ocean escorts. The British had a well-organized system for handling those movements and Admiral Layton proposed that it continue to operate independently and outside of the joint naval command which was about to be initiated. Admiral Hart stated that such a method would mean responsibility without commensurate authority and hence would be unacceptable to him; that, of course, for any measure taken toward guarding anything as important as troop convoys he would be most unlikely to disturb a going concern; but that he must have cognizance and full authority. There was considerable argument but Admiral Layton eventually conceded that Admiral Hart was correct.

With this meeting there began the personal conferences and cooperation which carried through during the interim up to the time that General Wavell assumed the full command of what became known as the "ABDA" (American-British-Dutch-Australian) area. Admiral Helfrich advised against setting up the joint naval command post elsewhere than at Batavia and Admiral Layton was disposed to agree with him.

On 10 January, General Wavell arrived by plane with several Army and R.A.F. staff officers. A general conference was held that afternoon at which General Wavell expressed some general views, quite simply and directly, and set forth the situation in Burma and Malaya, rather optimistically. The various conferees were called upon to state their views. Admiral Layton had little to say except as regards escort and convoy of reinforcing troops and materials through the Soemba Strait to Singapore. Admiral Helfrich expressed considerable optimism over the prospects of combined cruiser and destroyer operations, with all available ships, against the enemy's expeditions. Admiral Hart pointed out, on that subject, that IF the enemy controlled the air over the sea areas his surface forces would have the advantage of better information about our forces than ours would have of his; that, in addition our surface forces would have to cope with air attack – which they would do but that we should be realistic in measuring those disadvantages.   Admiral Hart expressed his belief that the cooperation of ships and planes, including land-based planes, was of even more importance than the cooperation between troops and planes – to which view no exception was expressed. Admiral Hart also stated that thus far the submarines, though inflicting damage on the enemy's amphibious expeditions, had not succeeded in breaking any of them up; and he finally pointed out that it remained to be decided how much of the effort of the Allied cruisers and destroyers was to be devoted to striking forces and how much to protecting convoys. General Wavell – at this or perhaps a later conference – said that the two missions were of about equal importance, that at least the convoy-escort task was not secondary.

The supreme commander then said that his short title would be "ABDACOM" (American-British-Dutch-Australian Command) and announced similar titles for his subordinates, including "ABDAFLOAT." He then stated that the GHQ would be at Lembang 10 miles from Bandoeng which was the secondary seat of the N.E.I. government. When asked his views about the location, Admiral Hart stated that there were objections to placing a naval command post up in the hills where the officers of ships could not reach it, etc. But, that since a combined headquarters was wanted, the only proper course was to try it – which ABDAFLOAT would be prepared to do as soon as rapid communications could be assured.

ABDACOM then presented the outline of his command and staff organization, all of which, including assignments of individuals, had been decided upon before his arrival in Java. There were to be five sections:

- Intendant General: Lt. Gen. Brett, U.S.A.
- Intelligence: Col. (Leonard F.) Field, R.A.
- Navy (Operational Command): Adm. Hart, U.S.N.

- Air (Operational Command): Air Marshal (Richard E.C.) Peirse, R.A.F.
- Army (Operational Command): Lt. Gen. (Hein) ter Pooten, N.E.I.A.

The air marshal was still in Britain. General Brett was to take over this command in the interim, as additional duty; he was also the deputy ABDACOM and was, in consequence, bound to be seriously overloaded. The chief of staff was Major General (Henry R.) Pownall, R.A., recently CinC, Malaya, vice Brook-Popham. His chief of staff in that latter billet, Major General (Ian S.) Playfair, R.A., was assigned as chief of staff to General ter Pooten; the latter continued to actively command his own army and was at GHQ for only a brief period each day, at the most.

After the conference, Admiral Hart gave Admiral Helfrich an opportunity to assign his own chief of staff, Captain (J.J.A.) Van Stavaren, as chief of staff to ABDAFLOAT. Admiral Helfrich replied that he could not spare Van Stavaren, whereupon Admiral Hart announced that he would take Rear Admiral (Arthur Francis) Palliser, R.N. The latter had come out as chief of staff to Admiral Tom Phillips but had just taken over the British navy command at Batavia; he was immediately relieved as such by Captain (John A.) Collins, R.A.N. – Admiral Layton's war plans and operations officer.

Admirals Hart and Layton received despatches from their respective governments asking their opinions on the qualifications of Admiral Helfrich for the command of the joint naval forces and both replied favorably – on the 11th. Admiral Helfrich expressed his dissatisfaction with his own prospective position as a relatively subordinate commander, in an echelon below that of his own army vis-a-vis, General ter Pooten: Admiral Hart immediately communicated the above facts, and everything else which he knew about this subject, to General Wavell.

A second full conference was held at Batavia, by ABDACOM, during the afternoon of the 11th at which the principal business was on details and arrangements for setting up the command post. ABDAFLOAT reported the formation of his operating staff – one captain and one commander from each of the three fleets – and that he would be prepared to shift to Lembang as soon as the considerable arranging of communications was completed.   He   reiterated his views about ship-plane cooperation, in view of the inclusion of all aircraft under one, (R.A.F.), command. Incidentally, Captains (Frank) Wagner and (Felix) Stump had been called to Batavia in order to have them on the spot and available for the reconnaissance command.

Up to this point the major point of discussion and consideration within the ABDACOM staff had been the Malaya campaign and the arrival of reinforcements, looking forward as far as two months. Little thought was expressed about the eastern half of the ABDA area and the speed at which amphibious warfare progresses seemed not well realized. The Japanese jumped off from Jolo and Davao and landed at Tarakan and Menado on 11 January. This was the first blow against the N.E.I. The event did direct more attention toward the eastern part of the theater.

Working conditions at Batavia were being very difficult for the British and Americans and getting things done took undue time and effort.

The Japanese rapidly completed their occupation of Tarakan and of Menado and the vicinities of both. At Menado they made their first use of paratroops, which seemed to work but there was little opposition. The Dutch reported that they did a good job of destruction of the petroleum installations at Tarakan. These two enemy operations well illustrated the methods which all their amphibious expeditions followed:

The expeditions formed at Jolo and Davao, at both of which points landing fields were seized and prepared. From those fields the first step was to use their navy planes to knock out the Allied aircraft, over the country and the landing fields in the general vicinity of the next objective. That accomplished, the troops followed, guarded by numerous anti-submarine craft and strong forces of surface ships. The troops usually constituted a divisional organization and they were equipped for beach landings; apparently the Jap expeditions generally did not have to depend upon wharves and alongside unloading even for the heaviest equipment which they used. After seizure of a port, the next step of the enemy was to repair its air fields and move his own aircraft in on them, in preparation for the next advance.

The Allied fleets continued the operations of the preceding period and two important convoys were passed into Singapore. General Wavell, who was at Singapore 13-14 January, finally took over formal command of the ABDA area on the evening of 15 January. Up to that time, the three fleet commanders continued to work at Batavia, on the cooperative principle. There was always agreement in the end but frequently preceded by efforts to "get the others to do it." It was plainly difficult for the British flag officers to relinquish control but their attitude was correct. Admiral Layton departed, (16th). No information came from Washington about prospective reinforcements. The commanding general USAFFE sent ABDACOM additional despatches about supplying him at Corregidor. The installation of a communication system from Lembang was proving very slow and the move to the new GHQ was being delayed in consequence. In the meantime, it was difficult to carry on the work from Batavia.

On 14 January, CinCAF ordered his forces to make a cruiser-destroyer night attack on Kenia which, it was learned, was being used by the enemy ships of the expedition which took Menado. The striking force (destroyer torpedoes were to be the primary weapon), formed up quickly and made two-thirds of the long run, through unfamiliar and narrow waters, when it received word from a U.S. submarine that the enemy had moved out of Kema and the vicinity. This was the first one of several attempts of the sort. H.M.S. *Jupiter* sank a large enemy submarine southwest of Java on the 16th; recovered two prisoners.

Although by the end of this period ABDAFLOAT was in full operational command the cooperative principle had carried over and to some extent that condition obtained throughout.   This fact was fully realized, and it was believed the correct way. Rear Admiral Palliser was chief of staff and he was also the best informed concerning the state of the British naval forces and of its shore installations. It was therefore natural that his advice should carry great weight and   to permit him to make all minor decisions concerning the British, including the actual arrangement of convoys. It is considered that Admiral Palliser was truly loyal. For instance, some time after arriving at Colombo, Admiral Layton attempted to withdraw the four best British destroyers from the ABDA area; he had certain valid grounds upon which to make that attempt. It would have been a serious error – at the time – as Admiral Palliser saw at once and he valiantly fought out the question on which, in the end, he won. Admiral Hart similarly handled the U.S. naval forces – quite directly.

It was at least from the political and psychological angle, advisable to, similarly, give Admiral Helfrich as much latitude as possible as regards his own forces and it was done as far as minor operations were concerned. The Dutch surface ships continued in use in covering the Singapore convoys for the remainder of January. As will appear later there was one occasion when Admiral Helfrich permitted a misunderstanding that had a serious aspect. At the time it looked as if the basis for it lay in language difficulties. However, there is one circumstance which requires recording:

Admiral Helfrich had long worked in a dual capacity for he was, in effect, the minister of marine to the governor-general, N.E.I. As such he was really a cabinet officer with much to do concerning N.E.I. merchant shipping and commerce and there was a political tinge to those duties. Admiral Helfrich was also the commander of the fleet which, incidentally had a different status from the army of the N.E.I., in that the fleet was "Royal" and the army "Territorial." It was rather natural for Admiral Helfrich to be somewhat dual in his attitude toward the Allies because of these circumstances. He was always under the governor-general's authority and was required to inform him on everything he knew, including secret ship movements, in consequence or which there was danger or compromise.

In his relations as a subordinate commander under ABDAFLOAT, Admiral Helfrich at times seemed to be motivated somewhat from the political angle and at other times altogether from the standpoint of a naval commander in war. At times he would be entirely frank and open in any matters which were under discussion, while at other times he acted more as in a civil capacity. The difficulty was that in the latter role, he seemed to wish to get naval forces other than his own to take on an undue proportion of escort duty and anti-submarine work in connection with the relatively unimportant movements of Dutch merchant shipping. The last conference with Admiral Helfrich prior to ABDAFLOAT's departure for Lembang, from Batavia, was entirely satisfactory and in a spirit of full frankness. Upon the whole that condition continued.

18 January 1942

On this date, ABDACOM moved from Batavia to Lembane into a mountain-resort hotel which is ten miles north of Bandoeng. The choice of location there, rather than in or near Bandoeng, lay in the idea of spreading out and, consequently, the better concealment of the GHQ from the air. Facilities were far from adequate, but upon the whole were good enough, with the exception of radio and land wire communications; (they improved as time went on, in consequence of much work, including addition of temporary buildings).

ABDACOM had a very complicated command involving four army, four navy, and six air organizations. Consequently, there was a great deal to do in organizing and equipping a GHQ, which naturally required time. In the face of an advancing enemy there of course was not time. The command function had to be exercised; but we never reach a condition under which it could be so exercised that there would be certainty that information and clear directives would be transmitted with despatch.

Despite the period over which the move from Batavia was delayed in the interest of establishing communications, those facilities were still quite unsatisfactory. In the first place, the equipment and the methods for rapid communications within the N.E.I. had always been rather limited – sufficient for their own purposes but very difficult of expansion.

ABDACOM's GHQ was set up with the idea that the codes and ciphers would be mainly British, but using Dutch equipment and channels as much as was necessary. Inasmuch as CinCAF still commanded his own forces at this time, (through his chief of staff at Surabaya), a navy radio unit and coding board was set up at Lembang. However, these units had to be retained throughout and were an important part of ABDACOM's communication system. Without their services, communications with ships would have been very slow and hopelessly glutted. The navy communication system was called upon to do much for the U.S. Army forces, which in the beginning had none of their own. The mass of army communications became so great that we were obliged to restrict and force them into N.B.I. commercial channels in order that navy   personnel could keep their own heads above water. Also, there was much danger of incurring compromise by handling army traffic.

By this time it had become apparent that ABDACOM and his immediate advisors, who were mostly of the British army, was still thinking mainly of Malaya (Singapore), and somewhat of Burma.

ABDACOM had not shown much interest when I discussed our eastern areas and the dangers of enemy penetration to the Malay Barrier on that side. As for the naval side of things ABDACOM's interest was primarily the safety of the reinforcing convoys going into Singapore. His trend was to promote employment of cruisers and destroyers on that mission without great thought to the consequent weakening of any possible striking force. At the same time, he was amiably critical of deficient naval opposition to the direct advance of the enemy's amphibious expeditions.

ABDACOM's set-up for air operational command called for an air marshal, (Peirse), to head the unified air command which had to control the six air organizations. The officer chosen had to come out from England; in the interim, General Brett, with General Brereton assisting, exercised such command as existed. General Brett being also the intendant general as well as deputy ABDACOM, was over-loaded – particularly since he had to pay considerable attention to U.S. Army affairs in Australia, with which he had been charged prior to the inception of ABDACOM. However, his actual air command duties during the period, (additional to work in connection with U.S. Army air reinforcements coming through Australia), was mainly confined to handling his own small detachment of heavy bombers. The R.A.F. air was all in Malaya and being directly commanded from Singapore. The immediate concern of CinCAF, as regards air, was the efficient operation of reconnaissance over water, for which his own remaining planes, with tenders, were available in addition to an approximately equal force of Dutch seaplanes. That particular air function was concrete, somewhat separated from the rest, and in the interest of best use for naval purposes, it was so maintained. General Brett at first chose Captain Wagner, U.S.N., to command the American and Dutch seaplanes; but eventually, and incident to Dutch opposition, he had to change that and put the head of the Dutch naval air service in command. However, Captain Wagner was kept in the reconnaissance command post, (at Bandoeng), as deputy, and the joint operation of seaplanes was carried on quite efficiently throughout. Captain Wagner had his three small seaplane tenders which were invaluable in providing flexibility of basing and, consequently, was in a strong position in his associations with the Dutch naval air.

The air reconnaissance command was established well ahead of anything else, had its own communication system, and, in general, its performance was better than that of the other air units seemed to be.

During the period the British army and R.A.F. were being defeated and pressed southward in Malaya at a discouraging rate, ABDACOM visited Singapore and also Rangoon, (two separate journeys). His absence on journeys of that sort seemed to create the impression that he was not taking enough interest in the affairs of the N.E.I. This was unfortunate and was probably due only to suspicion among the Dutch, as Malaya was the principal fighting front at the time. While in British circles there was talk of their army being shoved all the way down to Singapore Island and of an evacuation of Malaya by the R.A.F., the opinion was repeatedly expressed that Singapore itself would hold out indefinitely, even if the dockyard and port could not be used at all by our shipping.

We completed assembly of the ABDAFLOAT staff with Rear Admiral Palliser, R.N., as chief of staff, and with two British, two American, and two Dutch assistants – all of command rank. Additional to them was Lieut. Commander (Redfield) Mason, U.S.N., who, next to Colonel Field had come to be the most important member of the Intelligence Section. It had already become apparent that, other than by direct observation by reconnaissance planes, we would be getting very little information about the enemy from sources other than Corregidor. The naval unit there continued to be of the utmost value, and without its services ABDAFLOAT would have had to carry on very much in the dark. The American naval communication unit at Lembang increased in importance and grew to a total of something over twenty officers and men.

During the period, the Japanese continued some activity in the Molucca Strait but its character was not clear. There were signs of a build-up and of activity toward Ambon and Kendari but there was insufficient information for proper estimate of enemy intentions. I advised ABDACOM that the fleets could not be depended upon to break up an expedition against Ambon. I said that it would be well covered by submarines but that previous experience showed that they could not be relied upon to do <u>enough</u> damage to break up an expedition embarked upon in many ships, according to the usual Jap practice; and that only under an unusual coordination of favorable circumstances could we hope to get the few American surface ships available into action against the transports <u>before</u> they discharged. I also stated that if ABDACOM intended to withdraw the troops from Ambon he should act in the near future. The impression was gathered that the forces at Ambon should remain there and "fight it out".

The enemy completed his capture and occupancy of Tarakan and advanced south through Macassar Strait to Balikpapan, which he occupied without much opposition on the land. The Dutch reports were to the effect that all of the oil industry installations at both those places which were above ground were totally destroyed; moreover, that some or all of the wells were so plugged that the enemy would have to start drilling operations from the beginning in order to get fuel out of the fields. The demolition job at Tarakan was a smaller task than at Balikpapan but more time was available at the latter port, where the demolition began sometime before the Japanese appeared. While there is no doubt that the Dutch did accomplish a great deal of destruction at those places, we can by no means be certain that Dutch wells of considerable capacity did not fall into the hands of the Japanese. In any case, at Tarakan, which field gives a very high grade of petroleum, the oil is not at great depth. (Incidentally, the British field at Seria is said to be a very extensive one and the oil is very near the surface. In that field also, the oil is of a very high quality – good enough for boiler fuel as it comes from the ground.)

CinCAF had long believed that as far as natural resources were concerned, the oil fields were by far the most important strategic factor in the entire Far East area. On the possibility that the Japanese might capture some of the oil-bearing territory, CinCAF had urged the fullest possible preparations for destruction and had continued to press in that way insofar as befitted his position. Soon after the outbreak of war, he suggested that a certain amount of plugging of wells be started at once. There had seemed to be more reluctance on the part of the British owners of the Miri-Seria are than by the others. It was evident that very little preparatory work was done at Miri and Seria until the matter was finally put into the control of the British commander-in-chief, Eastern Fleet, in the autumn of 1941.

The striking force, (American cruisers and destroyers), jumped off on 21 January to attack into Macassar Strait. The movement was based upon a Dutch army report which was incorrect for the Jap advance was not made until later. This false move threw the striking force badly out of gear – burned up a lot of fuel, *Marblehead* developed defects on one shaft, and *Boise* was lost to the Asiatic Fleet for the remainder of the campaign by striking an uncharted pinnacle rock which ripped a long gash in her bottom near the keel. There was incomplete recovery of readiness to strike when the Jap expedition did proceed to Balikpapan.

However, four destroyers did attack off Balikpapan during the night of 23-24 January, with no loss, and succeeded in doing much damage. The results cannot be known but the destruction of four large valuable ships is certain and that of four others is most probable. The destroyers made either five or six known torpedo hits and between thirty and forty 4-inch hits at close range generally along the waterline, with the projectiles exploding inside, and known to have started some fires. As far as the division commander knew, he was in the presence of superior enemy forces. He ran past four powerful Jap destroyers, and our destroyers held full speed during the 1 ¼ hours that they were weaving in and out of the Japanese transport formation. In consequence, there were many misses by torpedoes which were launched at close range while passing the targets at high speed. The staff work which set up the attack, (from Soerabaya), was excellent; weather conditions fitted; the destroyers were efficient, and they were also lucky in that they suffered practically no damage. The Japanese expedition down the Macassar Strait also suffered from submarines and from the attack of Dutch and American army planes. The sum total of the damage inflicted proved to be such that the enemy stalled at Balikpapan and did not come farther by itself.

The S-36 was lost about thirty miles west of the city of Macassar, through grounding on an open sea reef, during thick weather. It should be said here that much of the waters of the N.E.I. are difficult from the navigational standpoint and since all aids to navigation had been discontinued as a war measure, the condition constituted a handicap at best. There was the still greater handicap or almost total lack of familiarity with the operating areas on the part or our personnel. The Dutch charts and sailing directions are much better than the English publications but our officers could not read them. Effort was made to supply the deficiency by obtaining pilots but the required Dutch personnel was said to be unavailable. Our surface ships had been nearly continuously at sea since the war began and the adverse effects as regards material efficiency or those old vessels were becoming apparent. Even when they were in port usually only a little could be obtained in the way of services. The tenders were at Darwin and their availability was reduced for that reason. The same circumstances existed for the submarines. Several of them were already several weeks out and, in fact, to find more than three or four in port at any one time was a rare occasion. It was well understood in our own fleet command that we were over-working our submarines, particularly for their first patrols, but so many emergencies kept developing on account of the necessity for resisting the enemy's southern advance to the utmost that there was nothing else to do.

Our submarines were continuing to shift their patrol areas to the southward in order to stay in front of the enemy advance. They continued, however, insofar as numbers available would permit, to patrol exits from the enemy ports and bases and to work on the enemy's lines of communications when information disclosed same.

It developed to be a mistake to have sent practically all our large auxiliaries all the way to Darwin, because that removed them so far from the center of gravity of operations or our ships which they existed to serve. A westward movement was consequently projected. During the period American destroyers sank a submarine off Darwin. Examined the wreck by divers, 165 feet of water, no opportunity to get detailed information.

Houston and two destroyers were being continually used in the Darwin-Torres Strait area for escorting American troop ships and auxiliaries. Also, we were having to meet some or the many demands for anti-submarine escorts in Java waters by using American destroyers.

Two more British convoys were sent to Singapore during the period and British and Dutch surface ships still were mainly engaged in that task. The Dutch surface ships remained fresh – not in overworked condition. The same condition applied to the Dutch submarines. They had been very active during December and two of them had sunk four ships each; three had been lost. But for some time the remaining Dutch submarines had operated most leisurely, usually with not more than two at sea at once.

During the period ABDAFLOAT visited Soerabaya in order to generally regain touch and also to arrange to bring Admiral Glassford on shore so that command could be turned over to him, as ComSouthWestPac, under conditions such that he could properly exercise that command. This was a difficult change to carry out in the face of an advancing enemy and was a subject of considerable embarrassment at the time.

Since about 8 January, there had been received several communications about getting supplies into the Philippines. At first it was a direct call, from USAFFE upon ABDACOM, in meeting which we sent anti-aircraft ammunition into Corregidor. Somewhat late but as soon as a cargo could be collected, a submarine carried small arms ammunition into Mindanao. This ammunition was sent in as soon as commensurate loads of the required components could be collected from Australia by our army authorities. A third submarine for which an ammunition load was not primary, also went to Corregidor from Java – somewhat later. These supply voyages of course took the submarines away from their primary war missions for considerable periods. However, this was not all loss from the strictly naval standpoint because upon their return the submarines brought out of Corregidor torpedoes, spares, and a certain number of key personnel, all of which was badly needed in the southern areas.

The project of getting food into Corregidor and Bataan was placed with the army by the President (Franklin D. Roosevelt), who made available a considerable sum to be employed for chartering merchant vessels and paying high wages to their personnel for attempts to run the supplies in from Australia or points along the Barrier. The naval authorities of all three nations in Java gave what assistance was possible but the full results are not known. CinCAF detailed a commander to assist our army authorities in Java.

The CinCAF also turned over to the Army a 2,000-ton freighter, (Filipino flag), which it had under charter from November, 1941, and sparked up the ship's personnel into full willingness to undertake the venture. This ship was the most promising of those which were heard of as employed on the project from within the ABDA area; but it is understood that the food components for her cargo were collected too late for the ship to get loaded and well started before the Japanese advance was pretty well on top of Soerabaya. She is understood to have been caught while still well south.

The most promising venture of the lot was another Filipino ship, *Don Isidro*, a fast diesel-engine inter-island ship which was sent south from Manila Bay during the early days of the war. This ship was loaded by the army in Australia in time to get through to the Philippines before the enemy had gotten very far into the N.E.I. waters. The CinCAF, after careful study, gave the ship a routing which seemed most promising; and involved going; through the Torres and Dampier Straits. Something miscarried, however, because the ship went south about Australia, to Fremantle, and was next heard of while approaching Batavia! *Don Isidro* was caught on the way north from there. Had she been properly directed for Australia, there was a very good chance that she would have reached Corregidor.

USS *Marblehead*

The returning submarines were by now reporting larger results than before but still were also reporting too many failures – warheads not exploding on hits, torpedoes missing on account of bad runs, and too many attacks failing for various other reasons. A considerable number of the failures was still the fault of personnel. As could have been expected, first war patrols of submarines are relatively inefficient and time is required to get into stride. The official reports of the Asiatic submarines will, for the most part, be available and should cover this subject thoroughly.

By this date, the submarines generally had been keeping the sea for unduly long periods; that is, upwards of 50 days for the large boats ad 30 to 40 for the small boats, all in tropical waters at that. Many of the patrols were much longer than was intended because, in so many cases, submarines which were on the way to base had to be turned back to increase opposition to the enemy's advance. It was being found, however, that, in spite of the very great hardships and strain over long periods, the personnel was standing it surprisingly well. Many were in rather bad shape upon return but appeared to recover in a very short period of rest.

CinCAF visited Soerabaya during the period and set up the new command arrangement under which he remained nominally CinCAF but with that office practically inactivated. Vice Admiral Glassford, with Rear Admiral Purnell as chief of staff, became commander, US. Naval Forces in the Southwest Pacific. The command post remained at Soerabaya but was tending to shift out of that city on account of the threat of the pending enemy advance. By now, the forces under commandant, Sixteenth Naval District, had officially come under USAFFE operational command; in practice, this arrangement had been in effect for some time. The Asiatic Fleet intelligence work did remain altogether under CinCAF and there was certain cognizance as regards communications but, in most all other respects, the naval and Marine forces, Manila Bay, were assisting the army. In this role their services are known to have been of great value.

During this visit at Soerabaya, it was seen that some days would elapse before an American striking force of much potentiality could take the sea; the destroyers had many empty tubes and no cruiser was available, except *Marblehead*, which was completing temporary repairs to main power plant. ABDAFLOAT visited Batavia upon return and conferred with Vice Admiral Helfrich and Commodore Collins, R.A.N. (He usually saw eye-to-eye with the latter officer and had come to rely very greatly upon his judgment and general attitude.) Vice Admiral Helfrich was still found disposed not to be entirely frank as regards the state and readiness of his forces. At this conference he did not disclose that he could get a considerable force of his own cruisers and destroyers to sea – which would have strengthened our current weakness to the eastward of Java. (Without information the ABDAFLOAT office, he had ordered these forces into the Karimata Strait. It was a proper action as instituted, but at the time of the conference the information upon which it was based had been found to be incorrect and the order had been cancelled. This latter was not disclosed for a little time afterward).

Started moving American auxiliaries westward from Darwin. (Directed it 29 January but first sailing was not until 3 February). This was necessitated by the requirements for servicing the destroyers and submarines in Java harbors. However, by now Darwin, as might have been expected, had been found most inadequate and unsuitable as a harbor and base. Moreover, being located in a bight of the ocean and free for approach from the north or west, it was becoming too easy for the enemy to cover Darwin and lock up anything inside. This decision amounted to our navy's moving toward discontinuance of the use of Darwin as a base and did not conform to the general attitude which the United States administration had adopted a month or more previously. ABDACOM did not personally approve of moving American auxiliaries away from Darwin but he accepted the idea since British and Dutch naval thought also agreed upon it.

At one of ABDACOM's conferences during this period ABDAFLOAT stated that the Allied naval forces could have accomplished much more in the way of direct opposition to the enemy advance if no cruisers and destroyers had been used for escort duty; that the past history showed that we would have lost nothing at sea if convoys had gone "bare" with the possible exception of one fuel ship, *Trinity*, which might have been lost in the vicinity of

Darwin had she been unescorted. Those statements were unwelcome but were true.

During the period, (29th), the decision was made by ABDACOM to concentrate the British army, which had been opposing the Japanese on the peninsula, on Singapore itself. Included in that decision was the virtual withdrawal of the R.A.F. from British territory and projecting its future operations from the air fields of Sumatra. Formal orders were issued closing the naval dockyard at Singapore, a step which was a very hard thing for the British to have to take in view of the Empire's policy over many years. It was understood that Rear Admiral Spooner, R.N., in command at Singapore, was himself considerably surprised at the suddenness of the British army's retreat. In consequence of the decision all ship movements involving Singapore now became a matter of bringing personnel and material out, rather than in, with general destination Java. Evacuation of women and children from Singapore had been in progress for some time but more or less on a go-as-you-please basis.

During the period, the Japanese were building up east of Celebes Island but their other expedition was still stalled off Balikpapan – where it continued to present some attractive targets. Preparations of American destroyers and *Marblehead* were pressed as rapidly as possible and *Marblehead* got out with four destroyers, (with some empty tubes, however), and made another jump-off into the Makassar Strait. However, they were shadowed by Japanese air during the afternoon and since it was a bright moonlight night the commander, very properly, decided not to drive home the attack in the face of the superior Japanese naval forces which air reconnaissance reported.

Chief Air Marshal Peirse finally arrived. ABDAFLOAT did his best to get on good personal terms with him, looking toward promoting cooperation between planes and ships, but never made much progress. The new air commander had not been trained for such cooperation. One of his assistants was Group Captain (Lawrence) Darvall, R.A.F., who had been long in Malaya; he was one officer of that service who seemed able to understand the problems over the water and, fortunately, he was available at the GHQ nearly all the time.

General Wavell again visited Singapore and upon his return stated in conference that he expected the island to hold out indefinitely though, of course, its port would not be usable. A Jap expedition attacked Ambon on the 31st and took the entire place within two or three days. The Allied air force still remaining there at the time was meager. The Dutch and Australian planes which had been stationed at the place had been well used up during preceding enemy air attacks. Our PatWing Ten lost two planes on account of inexperience – belonged to the squadron which had recently arrived. The Allies lost a strong battalion of Australians and some of the best units of the N.E.I. Army.

During the period, the Japanese remained inactive in the Macassar Strait. They continued to build-up in Molucca Strait and on the east side or Celebes Island – at Ambon probably but particularly at Kendari. There were very good Dutch landing fields at that point which had also been used by U.S. Army heavy bombers. They had hoped to continue such use and called for transportation of fuel supplies to that front. In compliance, 30,000 gallons of 100 octane gasoline were sent in by a destroyer plane tender which barely got clear just as a Japanese expeditionary force arrived to occupy Kendari. The navy did considerable running in order to lay down gasoline along the Malay Barrier for use of Army planes which were to be ferried from Darwin to Java.

Sent *Langley* to Freemantle to load Army P-40 pursuit planes, assembled under an agreement to transport them north if conditions were propitious when the ship was loaded and ready. In the interest of secrecy of the movement, requested army authorities to send no despatches whatever concerning this movement other than to direct that their planes be sent to Freemantle to be there loaded on a ship.

On 2 February called all three naval commanders, (Admirals Helfrich, Glassford, and Commodore Collins), to Lembang for conference with the objective of setting up a stronger striking force; most of the cruisers and destroyers were by then being relieved from escort duty into Singapore. Moreover, the enemy's next advance would be bound to bring his forces into easier reach o our forces, acting from the points from which they had to jump off. All the Dutch cruisers and destroyers had become available and there was prospect of soon using the British destroyers, of which two were very strong, modern ships; also there was possibility of using one, or even two, very good British cruisers, which were temporarily in the ABDA area.

During the conference, it was decided to set up the striking force with Rear Admiral (Karel) Doorman (Dutch) in command, with Rear Admiral Purnell as second in command if found advisable to have officers in the force. It was also decided to first assemble the force at sea, east of Java, as soon as possible and to strike at first opportunity.

The tactical handling of the mixed forces was discussed. Since there would be little or no chance for training, there were bound to be difficulties but it was held that they would not be great because the force would be small and the tactics simple. The ship-to-ship communications were to be by short-range, high-frequency voice radio. General Wavell looked over the agreements and approved. The striking force got assembled on the 3rd and was sighted that P.M. by enemy air units which attacked Soerabaya.

Soerabaya experienced its first bombing attacks on February 3rd and, according to the usual Japanese procedure, it was directed at the air installations. The Dutch fighters in the vicinity were beaten and mostly lost in the airs. The Japanese caught and destroyed a considerable number of planes on the ground, but all U.S. Navy planes got away. By then they had fully learned about dangers on the water, if they were where the enemy might expect them to be. The small airplane tenders permitted frequent changes of base – which was their salvation and permitted them to continue their invaluable reconnaissance work for so long in the presence of strong enemy forces.

On the 4th of February, the striking force was caught by a powerful Jap bombing attack while on the way out to a jump-off point for another attack. Two Dutch and two American cruisers, with a mixed force of ten destroyers, were in the formation. *Marblehead* was knocked out of the campaign by three bombs, and would have sunk at sea but for an unusually courageous and efficient personnel. *Houston* lost her after-turret and her main radio and had heavy personnel casualties – sixty killed. Both cruisers went to Tjilapjap. Admiral Doorman still had a considerable force intact, even after providing escorts for the damaged American cruisers, but he immediately withdrew all his ships to the south and west. That movement was not known at Lembang for over half a day on account of the very defective Dutch ship-to-shore communications. The striking force was, therefore, thrown out or taken out of action for the time being. Henceforth, the only American cruiser available in the area was the damaged *Houston*. The *Boise* sailed for Colombo 1-2 February. On 10 February, sent *Houston* on a troop escort mission, Darwin to Keopang. Although with after-turret disabled,

Houston was still the most powerful cruiser available in the area and quite capable of escort duty, at least. It was tentatively decided that when *Phoenix* arrived in the area, *Houston* would return to a home port.

This last jump-off of the striking force was about three days later than it would have been in the Dutch navy had acted with entire frankness in disclosing its state of readiness. The reason for such misunderstanding is still not known, but a natural tendency to hold back and expect American surface forces not to hold back had been more or less present for some time. I doubt that any individual is particularly to blame for that situation. Rather, it was a matter of failure to begin personal associations of American, British, and Dutch naval officials soon enough.

The westward movement of the striking force after receiving the bombing attack was, probably, quite unfortunate. It later developed that an enemy expedition had milled around in waters south of Celebes for nearly a day, 7-8 February, probably awaiting something. We had information of it – from patrol planes – but no surface ships were in position to strike it.

To 10 February 1942

During the period, General Wavell visited Burma and later Singapore. By the date of the latter visit, the Japs had already invaded Singapore Island and occupied considerable ground on its western end. ABDACOM directed four fast ships sent up to evacuate 3,000 R.A.F. personnel to Java.

The period was marked by an increasing number of Allied planes lost in the air. Most of the losses were British and it was said that nearly all of the 100 new Hurricanes which were gotten into action around 30 January, through risky and expensive movements of ships, had been "used up." U.S. Army and Dutch Army Air had also suffered and Allied power in the air was diminishing at an alarming rate. The reconnaissance command was also losing planes but was still keeping up a fairly good flow of information of enemy movements at sea.

During the period, ABDAIR disappeared from Lembang and was found to have established his command post at Bandoeng. This move was made without notice to ABDAFLOAT and when facts were made known to ABDACOM he indicated that he himself had not previously known of the move. There was continuing indication that the comparative weakness of the Allies the air had been more a matter of seasoned personnel than in an inadequacy of planes, in numbers or in types. This seemed to particularly apply to all squadrons of the R.A.F., and to the pursuit squadrons of the U.S. Army.

As soon as Admiral Doorman's withdrawal movement after receiving the bombing attack on 4 February was known, he was directed to reverse his movement and reform the striking force for use in the quadrant northeast of Java. He thereupon issued a directive setting up two rendezvous about 300 miles south of the Malay Barrier from which to fuel, assemble and jump off. This was a quite impracticable project in that the rendezvous were too far away and the sea there too rough for dependence on fueling at sea. Consequently, Admiral Doorman was directed to proceed to Tjilapjap for conference.

ABDAFLOAT visited Tjilapjap on the 8th, finding a considerable portion of the striking force in port, and conferred with Admiral Doorman.   The latter was found. to be rather over-apprehensive of enemy bombing attacks. Shortly after the meeting began information came in indicating a Jap expeditionary movement to be coming around the southeast end of Celebes and the island of Bouton. From previous information there was belief that the enemy's next move would be directed at Banjermassin, (southeast Borneo), or on eastern Java. (Actually, the enemy's next step was to take Makassar, 9-10 February). ABDAFLOAT represented in the conference that if such developed, at least a night attack must be made. He directed Admiral Doorman to draw up plans for it and to take up position in readiness as soon as it could be done. The plan was issued very quickly and ships of the striking force began leaving port; the plan was to assemble just south of the barrier and west of Bali. (By this time, it had become apparent that Admiral Doorman was naturally a very cautious sea commander and not inclined to take commensurate risks. Thought was given to relieving him but ABDAFLOAT decided against the step at that time. There was no cruiser available upon which to embark an American admiral and there was no British commander available; additional to which was the prevalence of feeling among the Dutch that their officers were not being given enough of the command positions, over the ABDA theater - in all areas).

At about the end of this period, there were indications of another Jap expedition forming. It was not ABDACOM's practice to keep up running estimates of the situation, or "appreciations" as the British call such documents. ABDAFLOAT kept up only very rough running estimates which usually were not preserved. On or about 9 February, the general strategic picture, as it appeared to him, was about as follows:

The British in Singapore had already been rendered innocuous and there was question of the destination of the new enemy expedition referred to just above. The indications were that it was being directed at Banda Island or its vicinity, with ultimate destination either western Java or central Sumatra, probably the latter.

There was at the same time to be considered the Jap movement through Molucca Strait; (and perhaps the remains of the detachment which came through Macassar Strait). It was known that the Japs had built up strongly around Kendarl and to the south of it, particularly as regards air fields and air power, so that it was a considerable base. That area having been relatively quiescent for some time, the assumption had to be made that there would be a push from those eastern Jap forces in the near future. While it later developed that they first made a short step only to Macassar, and generally occupying all of southwest Celebes, it was at this time estimated that a straight jump to Madura Island or Bali was quite likely. Also that if such jump were made, the striking force would have a fair opportunity for breaking it up. Unfortunately, for about 48 hours at this time, either bad weather or heavy enemy air opposition prevented our reconnaissance planes from getting any information. This fact caused ABDAFLOAT to hold to his estimate about 24 hours longer than would otherwise have been the case, during which time the striking force was retained to the eastward, whereas it should have moved west for use against the other invading expedition.

ABDAFLOAT also visited *Houston* and *Marblehead* at Tjilapjap on 8 February and saw at first hand the damage to *Houston* and *Marblehead*. Both ships had been severely punished, but the morale and courage of the officers and men seemed in no way impaired. It was finally decided that *Houston* would remain in the area for the present and that her next employment would be in covering a troop movement, which ABDACOM was forming up, from Darwin to Koepang or Timor, for the better protection of the landing field there.

Marblehead was seen to be badly wrecked. By virtue of a high degree of technical ability on the part of a Dutch naval architect, the ship's bow had been lifted out of water so that the hole in the bottom could be roughly patched. There was total lack of steering power but it was considered less risky to send the ship to sea steering with her engines than to attempt to get the stern out of water with the limited lifting power available in the Tjilapjap dock. It was decided that *Marblehead* must be gotten out of the ABDA areas early as possible, and she sailed for Ceylon, *Otus* accompanying, within

94

a very few days. Only unusually efficient and tenacious officers and men could have saved this ship in the first instance, or have continued to keep the sea with her over such long periods.

The tankers and tenders arrived at Tjilapjap and began giving long-deferred service, (including torpedoes), to destroyers and submarines which had long needed it. Thenceforth, Tjilapjap was the principal base for American ships; it was a most inadequate harbor but the only one with much of any security; said security lay entirely in the location.

The submarines continued to be active – Dutch boats in the western part of the theater, American boats in the central and eastern parts. Since their splendid performances during December, the Dutch submarines had not been effective. The American boats were by now bringing back larger "bags" than before and the total had become considerable. But there were still occurring too many lost opportunities to inflict severe damage on the enemy. It was still the case that the enemy could advance his amphibious expeditions in the face of submarines without suffering enough loss to stop or break him up. However, the submarines are thought to have caused the enemy greater losses than did everything else in the ABDA area.

During the period, the Japanese invasion of Singapore Island made ground very rapidly, against what was the equivalent of three full British divisions, and the surrender occurred on 15 February. During the last days of Singapore, evacuation of material and personnel – including women and children – was carried on as well as it could be done in the immediate presence of an invading enemy. Conditions were very chaotic. Ships of all types were subjected to considerable bombing attack, while loading and while at sea for quite a distance south of Singapore. The R.A.F. was operating from Java and the south central fields of Sumatra and offering opposition to the Japanese aircraft in their operations which began to extend well south of Singapore.

The Japanese invasion of the Palembang section of Sumatra got underway – a paratroop attack at first followed by landings on the east coast and movements up the rivers. The success or failure of this invasion was not clearly known in Java as the period closed. Neither was it known what steps, if any, had been taken toward denying the enemy petroleum from this, the most valuable oil property of the N.E.I.

There was a large influx of shipping into Java ports, particularly into Priok, the port of Batavia. Conditions had become badly disrupted at all the ports; their facilities would have been overtaxed at best, additional to which was the desertion of much of the Malay laborers as soon as they heard the first bombs explode.

The Japanese forces in Celebes and the surrounding territory made no move during the period. By the evening of 11 February, ABDAFLOAT decided that the menace to the west of Borneo was the greater and the striking force was directed to shift to the westward to oppose. As previously stated, about 24 hours were lost by the belatedness of this decision. However, the loss was more apparent than real, because when the striking force did jump off for the waters north of Banka Island(13th), Admiral Doorman had just been strongly reinforced by the addition of *Exeter*, *Hobart*, and most of the British destroyers. That made a force of four very good light cruisers adequately supplied with destroyers, and Admiral Doorman was in consequence told that "He should consider the advisability of an attack upon enemy expeditions by day as well as by night in view of the considerably increased power of his force."

The striking force got into the waters northeast of Banka Island during the night of 13-14 February, leaving one Dutch destroyer aground on the way. The force passed through several bombing attacks the next day without injury and then it returned to Batavia in the early morning of the 15th, having accomplished nothing. The Japanese expedition was already into Banka Strait, and the Sumatra rivers, with the advance elements of their expedition – with Palembang as their objective. The striking force arrived too late to defeat at sea the landing of the enemy's first waves, but it probably could have inflicted considerable damage had Admiral Doorman pressed into Banka Strait from the north or swept to the northward. There were several Jap detachments in the vicinity and there were some signs that just the appearance of the striking force in those waters considerably disrupted the Jap movements.

It became too dangerous to continue to send tankers into Palembang for cargo. The producing capacity on Java, which was all that remained available to the Allies was only 22,000 tons per month, which could be handled by a small number of tankers. Accordingly ABDAFLOAT ordered all tankers sent to the Persian Gulf as soon as they were ready for cargoes. He directed that the two American tankers be sent out as soon as practicable.

On 14 February, ABDAFLOAT directed that a large submarine be sent to Corregidor to evacuate the American high commissioner, the Honorable Mr. (Francis) Sayre, and four other civilians who were with him, and to fill the rest of the passenger capacity or the boat with naval personnel selected for their potentiality for carrying on the war.

On 12 February, ABDACOM received a directive under which Admiral Hart was to turn over operational command as ABDAFLOAT to Vice Admiral Helfrich. The turn-over was made on the 14th at Lembang. Admiral Hart represented to ABDACOM that with a Dutch admiral as ABDAFLOAT and a British admiral as a chief of staff, the American navy did not have at Lembang a representation commensurate with its power – which still was about half the total strength of the three Allied navies. Making no progress toward any remedial action in this line, he reported the facts to Washington but at the same time urged ABDACOM that Vice Admiral

Glassford be placed either in or near ABDAFLOAT's H.Q. This seemed very necessary in order that the Asiatic Fleet would have proper representation and have its interest and welfare looked after to the best advantage which seemed possible under the circumstances. Efforts of this sort, completing the turning over of Asiatic Fleet's affairs to Vice Admiral Glassford, etc., consumed the time up to late afternoon of 15 February, when Admiral Hart departed from Lembang bound for Washington.

THE END

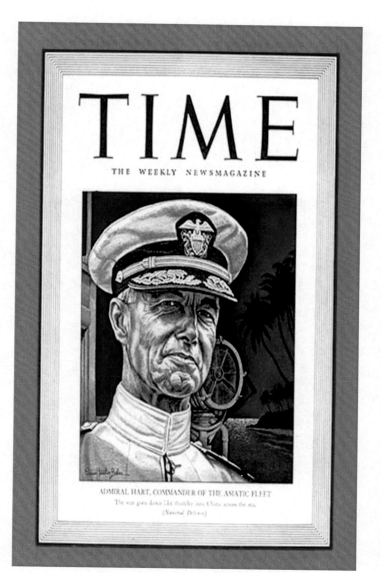

TIME

THE WEEKLY NEWSMAGAZINE

ADMIRAL HART, COMMANDER OF THE ASIATIC FLEET

The war goes down like thunder into Chêtu across the sea.
(*Neutral Debate*)

Made in the USA
San Bernardino, CA
22 March 2016